DATE DUE

	Kellykaughn		

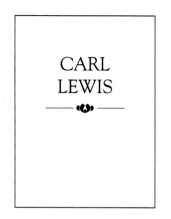

CARL
LEWIS

CARL LEWIS

Steve Klots

CHELSEA HOUSE PUBLISHERS
Philadelphia

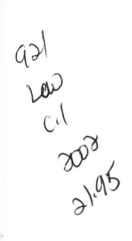

Chelsea House Publishers
Editorial Director Richard Rennert
Executive Managing Editor Karyn Gullen Browne
Copy Chief Robin James
Picture Editor Adrian G. Allen
Art Director Robert Mitchell
Manufacturing Director Gerald Levine

Black Americans of Achievement
Senior Editor Philip Koslow

Staff for CARL LEWIS
Copy Editor Catherine Iannone
Editorial Assistant Annie McDonnell
Assistant Designer John Infantino
Picture Researcher Pat Burns
Cover Illustrator John Weiman

The Chelsea House World Wide Web site address is
http://www.chelseahouse.com

5 7 9 8 6 4

Library of Congress Cataloging-in-Publication Data
Klots, Steve.
  Carl Lewis / Steve Klots.
    p. cm. — (Black Americans of achievement)
  Includes bibliographical references (p.) and index.
    ISBN 0-7910-2164-5.
       0-7910-2165-3 (pbk.)
  1. Lewis, Carl, 1961– —Juvenile literature. 2. Track and field
athletes—United States—Biography—Juvenile literature. [1. Lewis,
Carl, 1961– . 2. Track and field athletes. 3. Afro-Americans—Biog-
raphy.] I. Title. II. Series.
GV697.L48K56 1994   94-7347
796.42'092—dc20   CIP
[B]   AC

Frontispiece: *Anchoring the victorious U.S. 4 x 100 relay team,
Carl Lewis crosses the finish line
during the 1992 Olympic Games
in Barcelona, Spain.*

CONTENTS

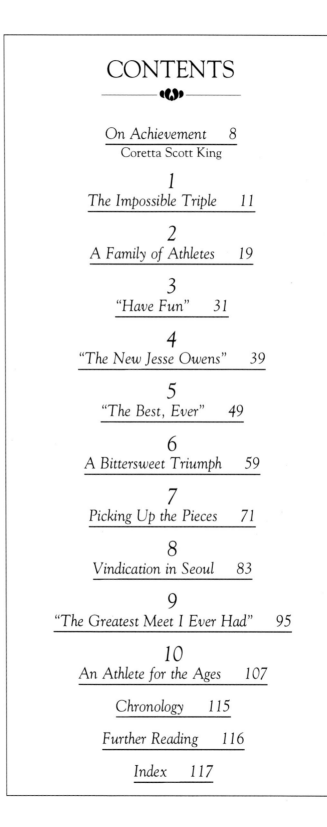

On Achievement   8
Coretta Scott King

1
The Impossible Triple   11

2
A Family of Athletes   19

3
"Have Fun"   31

4
"The New Jesse Owens"   39

5
"The Best, Ever"   49

6
A Bittersweet Triumph   59

7
Picking Up the Pieces   71

8
Vindication in Seoul   83

9
"The Greatest Meet I Ever Had"   95

10
An Athlete for the Ages   107

Chronology   115

Further Reading   116

Index   117

BLACK AMERICANS OF ACHIEVEMENT

HENRY AARON
baseball great

KAREEM ABDUL-JABBAR
basketball great

MUHAMMAD ALI
heavyweight champion

RICHARD ALLEN
religious leader and social activist

MAYA ANGELOU
author

LOUIS ARMSTRONG
musician

ARTHUR ASHE
tennis great

JOSEPHINE BAKER
entertainer

TYRA BANKS
model

BENJAMIN BANNEKER
scientist and mathematician

COUNT BASIE
bandleader and composer

ANGELA BASSETT
actress

ROMARE BEARDEN
artist

HALLE BERRY
actress

MARY MCLEOD BETHUNE
educator

GEORGE WASHINGTON CARVER
botanist

JOHNNIE COCHRAN
lawyer

BILL COSBY
entertainer

MILES DAVIS
musician

FREDERICK DOUGLASS
abolitionist editor

CHARLES DREW
physician

PAUL LAURENCE DUNBAR
poet

DUKE ELLINGTON
bandleader and composer

RALPH ELLISON
author

JULIUS ERVING
basketball great

LOUIS FARRAKHAN
political activist

ELLA FITZGERALD
singer

ARETHA FRANKLIN
entertainer

MORGAN FREEMAN
actor

MARCUS GARVEY
black nationalist leader

JOSH GIBSON
baseball great

WHOOPI GOLDBERG
entertainer

DANNY GLOVER
actor

CUBA GOODING JR.
actor

ALEX HALEY
author

PRINCE HALL
social reformer

JIMI HENDRIX
musician

MATTHEW HENSON
explorer

GREGORY HINES
performer

BILLIE HOLIDAY
singer

LENA HORNE
entertainer

WHITNEY HOUSTON
singer and actress

LANGSTON HUGHES
poet

JANET JACKSON
musician

JESSE JACKSON
civil-rights leader and politician

MICHAEL JACKSON
entertainer

SAMUEL L. JACKSON
actor

T. D. JAKES
religious leader

JACK JOHNSON *heavyweight champion*	MALCOLM X *militant black leader*	QUEEN LATIFAH *entertainer*	NAT TURNER *slave revolt leader*
MAE JEMISON *astronaut*	BOB MARLEY *musician*	DELLA REESE *entertainer*	TINA TURNER *entertainer*
MAGIC JOHNSON *basketball great*	THURGOOD MARSHALL *Supreme Court justice*	PAUL ROBESON *singer and actor*	ALICE WALKER *author*
SCOTT JOPLIN *composer*	TERRY MCMILLAN *author*	JACKIE ROBINSON *baseball great*	MADAM C. J. WALKER *entrepreneur*
BARBARA JORDAN *politician*	TONI MORRISON *author*	CHRIS ROCK *comedian and actor*	BOOKER T. WASHINGTON *educator*
MICHAEL JORDAN *basketball great*	ELIJAH MUHAMMAD *religious leader*	DIANA ROSS *entertainer*	DENZEL WASHINGTON *actor*
CORETTA SCOTT KING *civil-rights leader*	EDDIE MURPHY *entertainer*	AL SHARPTON *minister and activist*	J. C. WATTS *politician*
MARTIN LUTHER KING, JR. *civil-rights leader*	JESSE OWENS *champion athlete*	WILL SMITH *actor*	VANESSA WILLIAMS *singer and actress*
LEWIS LATIMER *scientist*	SATCHEL PAIGE *baseball great*	WESLEY SNIPES *actor*	VENUS WILLIAMS *tennis star*
SPIKE LEE *filmmaker*	CHARLIE PARKER *musician*	CLARENCE THOMAS *Supreme Court justice*	OPRAH WINFREY *entertainer*
CARL LEWIS *champion athlete*	ROSA PARKS *civil-rights leader*	SOJOURNER TRUTH *antislavery activist*	TIGER WOODS *golf star*
RONALD MCNAIR *astronaut*	COLIN POWELL *military leader*	HARRIET TUBMAN *antislavery activist*	

ON
ACHIEVEMENT

Coretta Scott King

BㄷFORE YOU BEGIN this book, I hope you will ask yourself what the word *excellence* means to you. I think that it's a question we should all ask, and keep asking as we grow older and change. Because the truest answer to it should never change. When you think of excellence, perhaps you think of success at work; or of becoming wealthy; or meeting the right person, getting married, and having a good family life.

Those important goals are worth striving for, but there is a better way to look at excellence. As Martin Luther King, Jr., said in one of his last sermons, "I want you to be first in love. I want you to be first in moral excellence. I want you to be first in generosity. If you want to be important, wonderful. If you want to be great, wonderful. But recognize that he who is greatest among you shall be your servant."

My husband, Martin Luther King, Jr., knew that the true meaning of achievement is service. When I met him, in 1952, he was already ordained as a Baptist preacher and was working toward a doctoral degree at Boston University. I was studying at the New England Conservatory and dreamed of accomplishments in music. We married a year later, and after I graduated the following year we moved to Montgomery, Alabama. We didn't know it then, but our notions of achievement were about to undergo a dramatic change.

You may have read or heard about what happened next. What began with the boycott of a local bus line grew into a national movement, and by the time he was assassinated in 1968 my husband had fashioned a black movement powerful enough to shatter forever the practice of racial segregation. What you may not have read about is where he got his method for resisting injustice without compromising his religious beliefs.

He adopted the strategy of nonviolence from a man of a different race, who lived in a different country, and even practiced a different religion. The man was Mahatma Gandhi, the great leader of India, who devoted his life to serving humanity in the spirit of love and nonviolence. It was in these principles that Martin discovered his method for social reform. More than anything else, those two principles were the key to his achievements.

This book is about black Americans who served society through the excellence of their achievements. It forms a part of the rich history of black men and women in America—a history of stunning accomplishments in every field of human endeavor, from literature and art to science, industry, education, diplomacy, athletics, jurisprudence, even polar exploration.

Not all of the people in this history had the same ideals, but I think you will find something that all of them had in common. Like Martin Luther King, Jr., they all decided to become "drum majors" and serve humanity. In that principle—whether it was expressed in books, inventions, or song—they found something outside themselves to use as a goal and a guide. Something that showed them a way to serve others, instead of only living for themselves.

Reading the stories of these courageous men and women not only helps us discover the principles that we will use to guide our own lives but also teaches us about our black heritage and about America itself. It is crucial for us to know the heroes and heroines of our history and to realize that the price we paid in our struggle for equality in America was dear. But we must also understand that we have gotten as far as we have partly because America's democratic system and ideals made it possible.

We are still struggling with racism and prejudice. But the great men and women in this series are a tribute to the spirit of our democratic ideals and the system in which they have flourished. And that makes their stories special and worth knowing. •()•

1

THE IMPOSSIBLE TRIPLE

IN JUNE 1983, Carl Lewis, a 21-year-old sprinter and long jumper, traveled to Indianapolis, Indiana, from his Houston, Texas, home for one of the biggest meets of his life—the USA/Mobil Outdoor Track and Field Championships. At the same meet two years before, he had astounded the track world by winning the long jump and the 100-meter dash, and a year later he had repeated the double victory. Now he was hoping to accomplish something that had not been done in almost a century. He aimed to win the 100, the 200, and the long jump, a triple that some people felt was impossible in modern times.

The crowd buzzed with excitement on Friday, June 17, as the three-day meet began. Featuring some of the best athletes in the world, the U.S. championship was a track fan's dream. Olympic gold medalist and world-record holder Edwin Moses was competing in the 400-meter hurdles. Mary Decker, one of the world's best women's distance runners, planned to race in both the 1,500 and 3,000 meters. Evelyn Ashford and Chandra Cheeseborough were certain to challenge each other—and the world record—in

Carl Lewis streaks across the finish line to win the 200-meter dash at the USA/Mobil Outdoor Track and Field Championships in Indianapolis, Indiana, on June 19, 1983. By winning the 100-meter dash and the long jump as well, Lewis accomplished an unprecedented triple victory.

11

the women's 100 and 200 meters. But for most fans, including the gathered coaches, officials, and athletes, the one to watch was Carl Lewis.

A year before, in the 1982 Sports Festival held at the same stadium, Lewis had made a long jump that some witnesses estimated to be over 30 feet, well beyond the seemingly unchallengeable world record of 29 feet 2½ inches set by Bob Beamon in the 1968 Olympics—and Beamon had been competing in mile-high Mexico City, where the thin air provided less resistance to his jump. However, a meet official nullified the jump, ruling that Lewis had stepped beyond the board at the end of the runway—even though Lewis had not left a mark on the Plasticine strip used to detect such fouls in major competitions. Before the jump could be measured, the sand in the pit was swept, erasing the probable record.

A month before, in the S & W Modesto Invitational in California, Lewis had sprinted to victory in the 100 with a time of 9.96—one one-hundredth of a second off the world record set by Jim Hines at the 1968 Mexico City Olympics. Lewis seemed to be peaking at the right time, and he would be competing in a stadium where he had all but achieved his dream of a long-jump world record. Everyone wondered if this would be the meet where Lewis would finally show how far he could jump and how fast he could run.

The meet began with numerous preliminary heats in the 100 and 200 that eliminated the slower runners from the field. For Lewis, the idea was to run comfortably in the preliminaries—fast enough to guarantee his advance to the next round, but not so fast as to tire himself out. Entered in three events, each with preliminaries and finals, he had to conserve his energy. Lewis easily won his first-round race in the 100 with a time of 10.32, then won his 200 heat in 20.70 less than an hour later.

The day had started well. Lewis felt good, and the track seemed fast, "scary-fast," as he said in an interview. For a couple of hours Lewis rested, occasionally receiving a few words of advice from his coach, Tom Tellez, or from his parents, Bill and Evelyn Lewis, who made a point of traveling to the big meets from their New Jersey home. Around him, other athletes completed their preliminary rounds, including his sister, Carol, who was eventually to win the women's long jump. When time came for the qualifying round in the men's long jump, Lewis carefully measured his steps, a routine that enabled him to leap cleanly from the board at the end of the runway. On his first jump, Lewis flew through the air to a distance of 28 feet 7¾ inches, enough to ensure him a spot in the finals. Conserving his energy, Lewis passed on his remaining attempts and left to rest for the evening.

On Saturday, Lewis took his first gold medal of the meet, in the 100. Running against a persistent head wind, the 6-foot-2-inch Lewis was at a decided disadvantage and edged out Emmit King at the finish line by less than two feet. His winning time of 10.27 was slow, but it was enough to win. The victory behind him, Lewis left the stadium to focus on the long jump and the 200 finals, both scheduled for the next day.

That night, a series of storms ripped through Indianapolis, drenching the stadium, and Sunday afternoon failed to bring any relief. The air was warm and heavy, and ominous clouds loomed on the horizon. As Lewis prepared for the long-jump finals, it hardly seemed like a day for world records. In fact, meet officials switched the direction of the jumpers' approach in order to avoid a head wind.

Lewis planned to take only one jump—assuming it would be enough for first place—and save his energy for the 200, the event at which he had the least experience. The crowd hushed as he began his

Lewis soars to a distance of 28 feet 10¼ inches as he wins the long jump at the Indianapolis meet on June 18. Lewis's leap, the second longest in history, was exceeded only by Bob Beamon's 1968 Olympic record.

sprint down the runway. In his last few steps, he seemed to realize that he was racing beyond his carefully measured steps, and he shortened his stride. Hitting the board cleanly, Lewis soared, pumping his arms and legs through the air and landing smoothly in the pit.

The jump was legal—and long. The crowd held its breath while the jump was measured and roared when the result was announced: 28 feet 10¼ inches. Lewis had made the second-longest leap in history, the longest ever at low altitude.

Certain that no one would challenge him for the victory, Lewis could retire for the day from the long jump. But he lined up for one more attempt. He had been so close to the elusive world record, on a jump when his stride was off. It was worth making one more attempt. As thunderheads rolled above the stadium, Lewis took a long look down the runway, then began his approach, hitting his steps perfectly. The wind was well under the allowable maximum for a world record—in fact, too far under. At only .56 meters per second, it failed to give Lewis the extra lift that might have carried him over Beamon's record. Thus, his second attempt came in shorter than the first, but it still measured a magnificent 28 feet 7 inches.

An hour later, Lewis won his semifinal heat in the 200. After another 90 minutes, he lined up for the finals. With the finish line around a curve in the track, the 200 was not only twice as long as the 100 but an entirely different race. Lewis had lately been working on running hard and fast through the length of the curve. As he said to the press, "The way to run this wrong is to try to catch up in the stretch."

Though never known for his fast starts, Lewis exploded out of the blocks and jumped into the lead. Ten meters into the homestretch, he knew he had the race won. Looking back at the competition, he broke into a big grin and crossed the finish line with his arms held over his head, posting a time of 19.75

Lewis reacts to the cheers of the crowd after capturing the long jump at Indianapolis. Lewis's habit of exulting in his victories earned him the resentment of some fellow athletes, who accused him of being a hot dog.

seconds, just three-hundredths of a second off the world record. Speaking to the press about his unorthodox finish, Lewis said, "I was tired. I knew I had to stay relaxed. That was my way of showing the joy of what I do."

The hard work had paid off. Lewis had done something that many had thought impossible. He had won the national championship in the 100, the 200, and the long jump. But to his dismay, some people immediately focused on his failure to set a world record in any of the three events. Critics pointed out that if he had maintained form through the end of the 200, he almost certainly would have broken Pietro Mennea's world record of 19.72, set in Mexico City.

After the race, Lewis eventually conceded that his finish-line antics cost him the world record.

Because of his inexperience in the 200, he simply had not realized how fast he had been running. Had he known, he might have acted differently.

The harshest attacks of all came from those who felt that Lewis had expressed more than joy at the finish line—they believed that he had been hot-dogging and gloating over his victory. Said Edwin Moses, "I think he rubs it in too much. I could dog my competitors and make them feel bad, but I don't." Lewis's longtime rival Larry Myricks, who had lost to Lewis in both the long jump and the 200, told reporters, "There's going to be some serious celebrating when Carl gets beat."

In his 1992 autobiography, *Inside Track,* Lewis defended himself against these charges: "I wasn't trying to make anybody else look bad, wasn't even thinking about anybody else. I was just excited, the way anyone in my situation would have been."

The charges of hot-dogging were a harbinger of the controversy that has followed Lewis throughout his career. If the first quality expected from an American hero is humility, then Lewis was destined to have a hard time winning the hearts of the American public. But with his unprecedented triple victory, Lewis also proved that, personal shortcomings aside, he was one of the best track-and-field athletes in the United States. His success in Indianapolis was also a sign of bigger things to come. As he went on the win nine gold medals in the course of four Olympics, setting two world records in the process, Lewis established himself as not only one of the best athletes in the world but arguably the best track-and-field athlete of all time. ❧

2

A FAMILY OF ATHLETES

O N JULY 1, 1961, Carl Lewis was born in Birmingham, Alabama. His parents, Evelyn and Bill Lewis, had met over a decade before while both were enrolled at Alabama's Tuskegee Institute, a leading black university. Their marriage in 1953 had brought together two hard workers who were also great athletes, qualities that both wanted to pass on to their children.

A native Alabaman, Evelyn Lawler had grown up near Gadsden, in the northeastern corner of the state. Her father, Fred, worked hard to ensure his family's well-being, overseeing their work in the cotton fields at harvest time, but never letting his seven children skip school, even to work. Their education came first, and part of that education was on the playing field.

At an early age, Lawler discovered her athletic prowess. She and her three sisters, Freddie, Lurene, and Sue, played basketball at Carver High School, and she and Freddie also ran track, her father often driving the whole team to meets in his truck. Eventually, Lawler's hard work in the classroom and on the track paid off. She so impressed Major Cleve Abbott, the athletic director at Tuskegee, that he awarded her a scholarship. She was the first member of her family to go to college.

Between track in the spring, basketball in the winter, and her studies, Lawler stayed busy, but

Carl Lewis at the age of five months, photographed outside the family home in Birmingham, Alabama. When Carl was two years old, Bill and Evelyn Lawler Lewis moved their family to New Jersey, where they accepted jobs as high school teachers.

Bill Lewis during his days as a football star at Tuskegee Institute. Lewis also ran on the Tuskegee track team, until he quit after a dispute with his coach— the determination to be his own man was a trait he passed on to his son Carl.

the routine agreed with her. While majoring in physical education, she competed for the United States in the 80-meter hurdles in the inaugural Pan American Games, the sports competition in which athletes from every country in the Western Hemisphere compete every four years. Unfortunately, a leg injury prevented her from competing in the U.S. trials for the Olympics in 1952, where she would have been a favorite to win a gold medal.

Unlike his future wife, William McKinley Lewis, Jr., had grown up hundreds of miles from Tuskegee on the streets of Chicago, Illinois. Lewis had played football and run track in high school; like Lawler, he was the first member of his family to go to college. He met Lawler shortly after his arrival on campus, and the two young people quickly began dating. While at Tuskegee, Lewis excelled in football (eventually becoming team captain) and track, although he eventually quit the track team after a dispute with the coach. Soon after Lawler's graduation, she and Lewis married; he received his degree the following year.

The newlyweds both took teaching jobs in Montgomery, Alabama's state capital. Mack, their first child, was born in 1954, and Cleveland (whom everyone called Cleve) followed a year later. Carl was the couple's third child, and their only daughter, Carol, was born in 1963.

On the surface, life was good for the Lewises. They had good jobs and four healthy, active children. But Alabama in the 1960s was a tough place for any young black family that wanted to raise itself up in the world. Many southern whites were reacting violently to the black civil rights movement; the young daughter of one of Bill Lewis's close friends was killed in the 1963 bombing of Birmingham's 16th Street Baptist Church. The Lewises were deeply involved in the fight for equality. Both had marched with the

Reverend Martin Luther King, Jr., to protest discrimination in the South, and King was a family friend, having baptized both Mack and Cleve. But in late 1963, when Evelyn heard from her sisters Freddie and Sue about teaching opportunities in New Jersey, where both had moved, the Lewises moved north in search of a safer environment for their children.

The Lewises found teaching jobs at rival high schools in Willingboro, New Jersey. Willingboro was a tidy, integrated, middle-class suburb of Philadelphia, Pennsylvania. As Carl Lewis later recalled, "We were another middle-class American family, going to church, playing Little League, getting to know the neighbors, talking and laughing around the dinner table."

The Lewises were a close, loving family. Although they were not wealthy, there always seemed to be enough money to pay for such extras as theater tickets and music lessons; Carl grew up playing the cello and the piano. Carl and Carol were especially close. The two did almost everything together, so when Carl began playing the cello, Carol took up the violin. But the children also were taught to think and act for themselves. For instance, when the family traveled to Alabama to visit relatives, the children were given the money to buy their own plane tickets and were told to check their own baggage.

Not surprisingly, all the Lewises shared an interest in sports. When Evelyn Lewis began teaching at Willingboro High School, there was no girls' track team. The principal argued that there just was not enough interest. Lewis, however, wanted all girls to have the same opportunities that she had enjoyed growing up in Alabama. With the help of her husband, she started the Willingboro Track Club and signed up a dozen girls who were interested in running. Twice a week the group practiced at John F. Kennedy High School, where Bill Lewis taught.

Evelyn Lawler as a member of the track team at Alabama's Tuskegee Institute. A star athlete throughout high school and college, Lawler missed her chance to compete in the 1952 Olympics because of a leg injury—her son Carl would later make up for this by capturing nine Olympic medals.

Bill and Evelyn Lewis, shortly before their marriage in 1953. Intelligent, energetic, and talented, the Lewises inspired their four children to excel in every aspect of life.

Soon some neighborhood boys asked to join, and the track club began traveling to area meets.

Carl was only seven when his parents founded the Willingboro Track Club. He was too young to compete, but he was old enough to tag along. The long-jump pit became a sandbox for him and Carol, then five. While Mack, Cleve, and the other Willingboro runners practiced their sprints under the tutelage of the elder Lewises, Carl and Carol built sand castles, then destroyed them by jumping into the pit.

According to Carl, it was Carol who first noticed that running and jumping into the pit, like a real long jumper, could be fun too. Although two years younger than Carl, Carol was a precocious athlete who, at age six, was winning races against boys older than she was.

One day around this time, Bill Lewis had a pile of sand delivered to the house. He intended to use it to build a patio. Carl and Carol had other ideas and built themselves a homemade long-jump pit. Soon they were hosting a track meet for all the children in the neighborhood. They used chairs as hurdles and marked off distances for various races: the width of the backyard served for the 100-yard dash, and one lap around the house sufficed for the 440. Carl and Carol even awarded their mother's old track-and-field medals to the winners. When Evelyn Lewis discovered this, the meet quickly came to an end, and she spent the afternoon knocking on doors in the neighborhood to retrieve her medals.

As a youngster, Carl was different from the rest of his family. He did not automatically excel at sports and was, in his own words, the runt of the family. Mack Lewis, seven years older than Carl, was making a name for himself as a high school sprinter, setting the county record in the 220. Cleve took up soccer as his main sport and was later named to the All–New

England team at Brandeis University; in 1978, he became the first black American drafted by a pro soccer team, ultimately playing two seasons for the Memphis Rogues. Carol was smaller than Carl, but she was remarkably strong and fast.

Carl did not seem to have an aptitude for any sport. When he was eight, he tried playing baseball, but he found the sport too slow paced. Playing one day in a Pony League game, he was busy picking daisies in center field when a ball was hit toward him. His mind was far from the game, and he caught up with the ball only when it stopped rolling. In neighborhood pickup games, the diminutive Carl was often the last one chosen for a team, whatever the sport.

Despite his size, however, Carl refused to give up, and his parents encouraged him. In track, at least, Carl could keep trying to beat his sister. Finally, in 1971, Carl started running for the Willingboro Track Club in the Jesse Owens meets for novices in Philadelphia. As usual, he did not win a single event. But he met the man for whom the meet was named, a former Olympic star who foreshadowed all that black Americans have accomplished on and off the track through athletic prowess.

A native of Alabama like Lewis, Owens had been nine years old in 1923 when his family moved north to Cleveland, Ohio. Competing for Fairmount Junior High School, Owens discovered he had a knack for sprinting and long jumping, and he soon became one of the most talked-about young athletes in the country. As a junior in high school, he just missed winning a spot on the U.S. team for the 1932 Olympics, and by the end of his senior year, he broke or tied the high school world record in three events: the 100- and 220-yard dashes and the long jump.

After high school, Owens won a scholarship to Ohio State University. With the nation in the depths of the Great Depression, he was one of just a handful

American sprinter Jesse Owens wins the 100-meter dash at the 1936 Olympics, held in Berlin, Germany. Owens's brilliant performance in Berlin demolished the racist fantasies of Germany's Nazi leaders and made him a legend in the annals of sport.

of black students at the school. Nonetheless, the congenial Owens continued to excel in track and gained great popularity among his classmates. At the Big Ten Conference Championships in 1935, Owens put on what is arguably the best individual performance ever in a single track-and-field meet. In the space of 45 minutes, he broke five world records and tied another—despite having injured his back by falling down some steps a week before. Racing on a cinder track, Owens tied the world record of 9.4 seconds for the 100-yard dash and broke the 220 record with a time of 22.6 seconds; these times converted to world records in their metric equivalents. A few minutes later, Owens shattered the long-jump world record with a leap of 26 feet 8½ inches. In a day of unscientific training and crude athletic facilities, this was an astounding jump, a standard that would not be topped for 25 years.

Owens's greatest moment came in the 1936 Olympics, held in Berlin, Germany. Adolf Hitler, Germany's Nazi dictator, viewed the Olympics as a chance to prove his racist fantasies. According to Hitler and his Nazi party, Germans belonged to the so-called Aryan race, which was supposed to be mentally and physically superior to all others, especially Jews and people of color. In the months leading up to the Olympics, Hitler's supporters had lifted the German public into a nationalistic frenzy, and the expected coronation of Germany's athletes as Olympic champions was all that remained to be done.

Instead, Jesse Owens, the black American, made a mockery of the Nazis' propaganda. Running against Hitler's best, Owens first won the gold medal in the 100. Leading from start to finish, he tied his own Olympic record of 10.3 seconds, which he had set in the preliminaries. To the horror of the Nazis, Owens quickly became the toast of Berlin, as ordinary Germans expressed their admiration and affection for the fleet-footed and amiable American.

The next day, Owens barely qualified for the finals of the long jump. His first two attempts had been fouls. As he nervously awaited the third and final qualifying attempt, his main rival, Germany's Luz Long, approached Owens and, in broken English, spoke a few words of encouragement and advice. The gesture of sportsmanship gave Owens the necessary

Jesse Owens poses with Germany's Luz Long during the 1936 Olympics. As Owens and Long dueled for the gold medal in the long jump, they formed a personal bond that exemplified the Olympic ideal of sportsmanship.

focus, and on his third attempt, he broke the Olympic record, then ran over to thank Long.

The two athletes dueled like champions in the finals. Long fit the description of the typical "Aryan superman"—blond and blue-eyed, with a sculpted physique—but as he and Owens passed and repassed each other's best jumps, they cheered each other on to greater efforts. Finally, on his last attempt, Owens clinched the victory with an Olympic record leap of 26 feet 5⁵⁄₁₆ inches. The first to congratulate him was Long, who ran over and embraced the black American. The German crowd went wild.

Before the Olympics were over, Owens also won the gold in the 200, with an Olympic record time of 20.7 seconds, and ran a leg on the victorious U.S. 4 x 100 relay team. The victories brought his gold-medal total to four, a feat never before accomplished in a single Olympics. When Owens received his gold medals, Hitler refused to shake his hand. Newsreel cameras caught the jackbooted dictator turning away in disgust from the scene of his embarrassment—an image cherished for years to come by all those who despised the brutality of nazism.

Owens returned to the United States a national hero, at a time when some Americans refused to treat blacks as human beings. Unfortunately, he never had the chance to run in another Olympics. In 1939, Hitler's aggression touched off World War II, and both the 1940 and 1944 Olympics were canceled. But Owens's magnificence in Berlin in the face of Nazi propaganda, and his friendship with the German Luz Long, provided a standard of excellence and a testament to the human spirit that may never be matched. Owens became an American legend.

As Carl Lewis was growing up, other black American athletes emerged as role models, winning the praise and respect of the nation. Among them were Rafer Johnson, who set an Olympic record in winning the 1960 Olympic decathlon in Rome, Italy, and sprinter Wilma Rudolph, who won three gold medals in the 1960 Games. For any youngster interested in track during the 1960s, however, there was no figure more exalted or inspiring than Bob Beamon.

On October 18, 1968, Beamon found himself in the finals of the Olympic long jump in Mexico City. Conditions were perfect for a good jump. There was a gentle tail wind that could help lift a jumper into the air. More important, Mexico City was situated 7,349 feet above sea level (more than a mile high), and at such altitudes, the air offers less resistance to a hurtling body; several world records had already been set in the sprints.

But no one expected Beamon himself to do anything unusual. He had barely made the finals on his last qualifying attempt, having fouled in his first two attempts. Instead, long-jump fans looked to

Demonstrating his unorthodox style, Bob Beamon soars toward the long-jump pit during a February 1968 meet. Later in the year, at the Olympics in Mexico City, the slender Texan shattered the world record with a leap of 29 feet 2½ inches.

Ralph Boston of the United States and Igor Ter-Ovanesyan of the Soviet Union to duel each other for a new world record. The two had traded world-record jumps for the previous eight seasons; currently Boston held the mark at 27-4¾. Whereas Boston and Ter-Ovanesyan trained for the long jump with the intensity and precision of scientists, Beamon had a reputation for being almost sloppy in his approach. Sometimes, as he approached the pit, he was uncertain whether he would be leading with his right or left foot.

While Beamon stared down the runway for his first jump of the finals, bolts of electricity shot from the Mexican sky, as if some higher power were trying to charge the atmosphere with energy and excitement. Going faster than he ever had in his life, Beamon hit the board perfectly, soared magnificently, and landed at the far end of the sand pit. Even before any measurement, it was obvious that he had made an almost incredible leap. But the crowd, distracted by a preliminary heat in the 400, did not at first react.

Slowly, however, the stadium started buzzing. With the wind at the maximum of 2.0 meters per second, the jump would count. The judges measured and remeasured the distance, then posted the result. Beamon had jumped an extraordinary 8.90 meters, or 29 feet 2½ inches. He had broken the old world record by a staggering 21¾ inches—almost 2 feet.

While the packed stadium roared its approval, Beamon collapsed to the ground as if all his strength had gone into that one jump. Boston, Ter-Ovanesyan, and the other competitors could only pick him up, clasp his hand, and shake their heads in disbelief. Beamon's feat was comparable to a sprinter chopping a full second off the world record in the 100 or a distance runner taking 10 seconds off the world record in the mile. Finishing the competition was a mere formality; no one dreamed of approaching Beamon's record. "I was ashamed to jump," Ter-Ovanesyan recalled years later. "Bob had left us and gone on to a new world."

Bob Beamon never again jumped farther than 27 feet. But in that one electrifying moment in Mexico City, he leaped into the realm of sports mythology. Beamon went to Mexico City a mortal man and returned to the United States a legend on the level of Jesse Owens.

As an undersized youngster, Carl Lewis never imagined that he might one day aspire to such a status. As he grew older, though, his talent and his ambition grew with him. ❦

3

"HAVE FUN"

Carl Lewis at the age of 13, when he was an eighth grader at Willingboro Junior High School. Still small for his age, Carl was determined to make up for his lack of size with hard work on the athletic field.

Bill Lewis had met Jesse Owens during his own childhood, when the Olympic champion was working as a district manager for a chain of dry-cleaning stores in Chicago. Stopping by a local franchise, Owens had taken the time out of his busy schedule to show the neighborhood youngsters, including Bill, his sprinter's start. Decades later at the Jesse Owens meet in Philadelphia, the elder Lewis was delighted to introduce his youngest son to an American legend.

Owens had two words of advice for Carl that day: "Have fun." For little Carl, running sprints and jumping had to be fun, because for someone of his size it certainly held no glory. No matter how hard he tried, he could not win. The accomplishments of others seemed unreachable to him. One day, in the front yard of the family home, he measured out 29 feet 2½ inches, the length of Bob Beamon's improbable leap in Mexico City. For Carl, the distance was almost incomprehensible. His only standard of comparison was to think that it was even longer than a Cadillac.

Finally, in 1973, Carl won the long jump in a competition for 12-year-olds at a regional Jesse Owens meet in Philadelphia. Again, Owens himself was on hand. As Lewis later recalled, Owens told the other competitors, "You should learn a lesson from this smaller guy. He was determined and he really tried hard."

The win qualified Carl, along with Carol Lewis and several other members of the Willingboro Track Club, to compete in the national Jesse Owens meet in San Francisco. After a series of fundraisers—bake sales, car washes, and dances—and outright subsidies from the Lewises' teaching salaries, the club raised enough money for the long trip. "Carol dominated, taking first place in her events," her brother recalled. "I was just another kid who ran, jumped, and went home empty-handed." But the meet gave him his first taste of big-time competition.

Throughout junior high school, life settled into a regular pattern for Carl. During the track season, he long-jumped and sprinted under the watchful eye of his parents. After school, there were pickup games of soccer and other sports, with Carol inevitably tagging along. And when his older brothers started earning some spending money through part-time jobs, Carl decided he wanted to do the same. First he got a paper route, delivering the local *Burlington County Times*. Then he was hired to flip burgers at a McDonald's, a job he held until he got tired of friends coming in and putting in large, complicated orders just to confuse him.

Carl then enrolled at John F. Kennedy High, where his father taught social studies and coached track. At the start of the year he went out for the soccer team, but the coach, seeing his scrawny build, relegated him to the junior varsity. Carl had played on a Willingboro youth league team for years, and he led the jayvee squad in scoring, with 15 goals and 10 assists. At the end of the season, when the coach invited him to join the varsity squad for the remainder of the year, Carl refused, feeling that he should have been on the varsity for the whole season. In any case, he was ready to start focusing on track.

As the track season approached, Carl experienced what doctors call a growth spurt, gaining two or three inches of height in just a few months. For a few weeks he even had to go around on crutches because the ligaments in his legs had been stretched too suddenly. His legs hurt constantly as he competed, but he also started to win, as all those years of hard work as a "runt" paid off. By the end of his sophomore year, he long-jumped just over 22 feet, a fraction shy of the school record. When he entered the triple jump in one meet, he set a New Jersey state record for sophomores. He also began to gain speed in the sprints and hurdles.

Then his bubble burst. With three older teammates, Carl was running the shuttle hurdle relay, a race that requires a team to go back and forth twice

Willingboro High School, where Evelyn Lewis worked as a teacher and coach. When her son Carl transferred to the school as a sophomore, his athletic career took off.

Patsy Marino, Lewis's track coach at Willingboro High School. Marino and Lewis often argued over Lewis's insistence on following his own training methods. "I realized later Carl knew what he was doing," Marino finally admitted.

across a straight 120-yard hurdle course. For this particular meet, the race was being run on the grass infield of the track. Over the first three legs, Carl's teammates built up a seemingly unbeatable lead—until Carl ran the fourth leg. Not as strong as his teammates, and wearing spikes that were too short for a grass surface, Carl faltered over the hurdles, without any of the fluid speed that his teammates had shown. Because of Carl's poor performance, the Kennedy team lost the race.

Carl knew that the defeat was his fault. Neither his father nor his teammates wanted to hear the excuse that he had been wearing the wrong size spikes. But while his father went easy on him, his teammates berated him, saying he would never run on their relay team again. In his autobiography, Lewis recalled making two decisions that night. First, before the next school year he would transfer to Willingboro High School, which most of his neighborhood friends attended; second, when he got to Willingboro, he would work so hard that he would never "be humiliated on the track again."

That fall, Carl entered Willingboro High School, where his mother taught physical education and coached the girls' track team (the track club's successes had convinced the principal that girls could run). He promptly had the number 25 stitched to his jacket, for 25 feet, a distance he vowed to jump before graduating. Some people laughed when they heard this, but Carl's athletic ability continued to improve. At the junior nationals in Indiana, he jumped 24 feet 9 inches, finishing third and just missing out on qualifying for a team that competed against the Soviet Union's best young athletes. Soon thereafter, at the Eastern States meet, he jumped 25-3¼, easily achieving his stated goal.

On the track, Carl also continued to improve. Wanting to focus on the sprints, he made a deal with his coach that he would not have to run the hurdles if he ran the 100 in 9.5 seconds.

Meet by meet he inched toward his goal, qualifying for a national age-group meet in Memphis with a time of 9.6. At the Memphis meet, he pulled off a stunning personal double, running the 100 in 9.3 seconds and winning the long jump with a magnificent leap of 25 feet 9 inches.

These performances did not go unnoticed. By the start of Carl's senior year in high school, a steady flow of college recruiters came through the Lewises' front door. Carl received offers of money, trips, athletic equipment, even cars, all to sway his decision. In his autobiography, Lewis asserted that Jumbo Elliott, the legendary coach at Philadelphia's Villanova University, even offered to set up his parents with a sporting-goods franchise.

Before going on to college, however, Carl had to make it through his senior year at Willingboro, where he had met with a series of difficulties. That year, Willingboro had a new sprint coach, Patsy Marino. Increasingly, Carl found himself in conflict with Marino. Teammates would hear Marino yelling, "I am the coach, Carl! I—am—the—coach!" Carl, who had spent his childhood reading his parents' coaching manuals and track magazines, had his own ideas about conditioning, and he refused to listen to Marino when the coach tried to make the sprinters run long distances in workouts. In general, Carl refused to listen to anybody just because he or she was an authority figure; the person also had to make sense. Several years later, Marino was to say, "I realized later Carl knew what he was doing."

Carl faced an even more serious problem: the more he jumped, the more his legs hurt, particularly his right knee. When long-jumping, Carl planted his right foot on the board for the takeoff, and his jumping style put his knee through extreme duress.

A view of the gym at Willingboro High School. As a senior at Willingboro, Lewis was heavily recruited by college coaches who were excited by his track-and-field potential. His yearbook entry concluded with the following message: "Plans: Run Forever; 'I am Serious.'"

To lessen the stress, he took full jumps only in meets, working exclusively on his approach and his steps during practice. Even so, his knee would swell up again immediately after a meet. He was suffering from a condition known as patella tendinitis, or jumper's knee. Finally he taught himself to jump off his left foot. For a time this alleviated the problem, but soon his left leg also began to hurt. All he could do was jump through the pain and stay away from the long jump on off days.

Despite his pain, Carl had no serious challengers in his high school meets. He had a definite sense of himself and what he wanted to accomplish. When he thought of college, he wanted most of all a coach who could help him attain his long-term goals on and off the track. In the spring of his senior year, he narrowed his list of choices down to six schools, and he promised his family he would make a decision by

Easter. Heading the list was Tennessee, a traditional track powerhouse. But when his mother woke him up on Easter morning and asked him where he was going, he said, "Houston."

Tom Tellez, the Houston coach, had offered Carl only one thing in addition to the standard track scholarship—good, solid coaching. As an assistant at the University of California at Los Angeles, Tellez had coached several National Collegiate Athletic Association (NCAA) champions in the long and triple jumps. Now he was hoping to surpass that success as a coach at Houston. For the Lewis family, extra cash or a sporting-goods store would have been nice bonuses in the short term, but Carl decided to go with the school that he felt, in the long run, would make him a better sprinter and jumper.

With the decision made, Carl could focus on enjoying his senior year. In the New Jersey Grand Championship meet, he set a meet record in winning first place. The last highlight of his school career came the day of his senior prom. After a last-minute cancellation, he was invited to race the 100 in the Martin Luther King Games in Philadelphia. There, he went up against some of the nation's best runners, including Houston McTear, an NCAA champion from the University of Florida, and Steve Williams, who in 1976 had been the top-ranked sprinter in the world. Carl had a solid race and finished fourth. To his own astonishment, he even beat Williams, who had been one of his track idols. At that point, he promised himself that he would not keep running when he was past his prime.

Because of the meet, Carl was late for the prom. It was, however, a small sacrifice. Running in the Martin Luther King Games had given him a chance to prove to the world and, more important, to himself that he was ready for the big time. ◖◗

4

"THE NEW JESSE OWENS"

AFTER GRADUATING FROM high school in the summer of 1979, Lewis continued to improve. That summer he was named to the U.S. team for the Pan American Games in Puerto Rico, where he stunned the veterans of the track world by finishing third in the long jump, winning a bronze medal. He also took the bronze in the Spartakiade Games against the Soviet Union.

The day after he arrived in Houston, Lewis went to see Coach Tellez. By then he had met several members of the team, and he was genuinely excited to be a member of the Houston Cougars. After telling Tellez how glad he was to be there, Lewis brashly declared that he had some off-the-track goals too. "I want to be a millionaire," said Lewis, "and I don't ever want a real job."

Tellez politely ignored the comment. He was more interested in molding Lewis into a champion long jumper, and when practice started, he told Lewis to forget everything he had ever learned about jumping. If Lewis wanted to jump without destroying his legs, the coach said, he had to relearn the long jump.

Because of the patella tendinitis in Lewis's right knee, the muscles in his right leg had begun to atrophy. The fault lay in his method. In high school, Lewis had been a "hang" jumper. A jumper using this

Competing for the University of Houston, Lewis barrels into the long-jump pit at the 1981 NCAA Outdoor Championships. By winning both the long jump and the 100-meter dash, Lewis became the first athlete since Jesse Owens to capture NCAA titles in both a track event and a field event at the same outdoor meet.

method plants his foot on the board and pushes off, while swinging his body and arms forward. Although this style seems most natural, it has some drawbacks. First, the jumper is tempted to overstride in order to plant his foot squarely on the board, an error that will sometimes lift him high into the air without propelling him very far forward. Second, the jumper tends to put undue stress on his lead leg, especially when overstriding. For Lewis, the result had been the dangerous swelling and sharp pain in his right knee.

Tellez wanted Lewis to learn the double-hitch kick method of jumping. A jumper using this method does not so much jump and hang as run through the air over the pit, his arms and legs pumping until he lands. In addition, Tellez urged Lewis to practice his steps, the carefully measured approach to the takeoff board, so he would never be tempted to overstride and reinjure his knee. In order to take full advantage of Lewis's great speed, he also lengthened Lewis's approach.

Because Tellez could explain why he wanted Lewis to change, Lewis was willing to listen. "When you get a kid who was as good in high school as Carl was, and you tell him 'I'm going to change you,' you'd better know what you're talking about," Tellez later said, "and he'd better know what you're talking about, and he'd better have confidence in you."

For weeks Lewis did not jump at all. Tellez was determined to give his young star's legs a chance to rest, and the two spent their time making Lewis's steps perfect. Finally, and very gradually, they began working on the double-hitch kick. Lewis put the new technique to its first major test in the 1980 NCAA Indoor Championships, which were held that year in Michigan. He jumped 26 feet 4½ inches—shorter than his best, but better than anything he had previously done indoors. It was also good enough for his first NCAA title. A few months later in the NCAA Outdoor Championships, Lewis won again

with a personal best, a wind-aided 27-4¾. Because he also ran for the Houston sprint relay team, some sportswriters began to compare him to Jesse Owens.

Lewis's performances earned him an invitation to that summer's U.S. Olympic trials in Eugene, Oregon. After the Soviet Union invaded the nation of Afghanistan, President Jimmy Carter had decided that the United States would lead a boycott of the 1980 Summer Olympics in Moscow, the Soviet capital. Nonetheless, the trials were still held, with the idea that the U.S. team would compete in other international meets and receive the fanfare and honor of Olympic athletes at home.

As was their habit, Lewis's parents were on hand to watch him and his 16-year-old sister, Carol, who

Carl and Carol Lewis discuss their athletic plans with reporters during a 1981 press conference. After qualifying for the U.S. Olympic team in 1980, the talented siblings found themselves much in demand on the track-and-field circuit.

Lewis competes in the long jump at a 1981 meet in Rome, Italy, as a member of the Santa Monica Track Club. Though still a college athlete and technically an amateur, Lewis was able to earn substantial money by competing on the European circuit.

had also earned an invitation to the trials. With the top three in each event making the team, Carl finished second in the long jump, losing only to Larry Myricks, who was ranked first in the world. In the 100, he finished fourth, good enough to earn him a spot on the 4 x 100 relay team. Making the team was an honor, but his biggest thrill came when Carol finished third in the women's long jump and also became an Olympian.

At the trials, Coach Tellez introduced Lewis to Joe Douglas, who had founded the Santa Monica Track Club in California in 1972. Although Douglas at that time primarily worked with distance and middle-distance runners, he invited Lewis to join the Santa Monica club, which was one of the up-and-coming forces in track and field. Lewis would compete for Santa Monica unless obligated to run for Houston or the American team.

Suddenly, Lewis was a hot property. His NCAA victories and selection for the Olympic team had given him immediate access to one of the least publicized aspects of international track and field—money. Since December of the previous year, Lewis had been under contract to Adidas; in essence, the shoe company paid him to wear its gear. Because of his performance in Eugene, Adidas gave him a large bonus; in time, Lewis would switch to Nike because of a contract dispute with Adidas. More important, through Joe Douglas he now had access to the financial rewards of international track and field.

That summer, Lewis ran on the European track circuit for the first time. In a few meets he competed for the American team with his sister, and sometimes he ran for the Santa Monica club. Running as a Santa Monica athlete, he received $300 to $400 per race, all paid under the table. Technically, international track and field was an amateur sport, and in Lewis's case, he was still an NCAA athlete and prohibited from accepting appearance or award money. However, he was by no means unique. His roommate on the European tour was Stanley Floyd, a star sprinter at Auburn University who was also paid to run.

In the fall, Lewis returned to school at Houston. Like any college sophomore, he had to choose the course of study he wished to pursue as a major. For a time he contemplated a degree in business. But after taking a speech class that he especially enjoyed, Lewis decided to major in communications, focusing on radio and television. He felt that this change would complement his athletic career: he could work as a sports commentator in the off-season while he was competing and then move on to a full-time job behind the microphone.

In any event, Lewis knew he needed to become a better public speaker. Whenever he had won a meet in high school, he had only had to smile as he accepted his trophy. But at the end of his senior year, he had been named state Long Jumper of the Year. When asked to say a few words at the awards ceremony, he had barely been able to stutter his thanks. Now the press was regularly asking him for interviews. In his view, a champion had to excel off the track as well.

By his own admission, Lewis was not the best student at the University of Houston. But he did take his classwork seriously, and he enjoyed his time at the university. Between his summer track earnings and his new contract with Nike, Lewis had the money to enjoy Houston's social life. As an added bonus, his brothers, Cleve and Mack, had also moved to Houston. Cleve took a job as a financial analyst, and Mack enrolled in the university to get a degree in geography.

Throughout the fall of 1980, Lewis slowly built up strength for the indoor and outdoor track season. As he grew more comfortable with the double-hitch kick method in the long jump, he was able to spend more time practicing the sprints. Once competition started, he began breaking records. At the February 1981 Southwest Conference Championship in Fort Worth, Texas, he exploded out of the blocks in the 60-yard dash to win in 6.06 seconds, the fourth-fastest time ever run. Moving on to the long jump, he broke the indoor world record with a magnificent leap of 27 feet 10¼ inches.

Although Lewis was still a foot short of Bob Beamon's record, the mark no longer looked so unbreakable. A few weeks after the SWC meet, in the NCAA Indoor Championships, Lewis won both the long jump and 60-yard dash, his third and fourth NCAA titles.

In June, when the 1981 NCAA Outdoor Championships began at Baton Rouge, Louisiana, the eyes of the track world were on Lewis. No one since Jesse Owens had won NCAA titles outdoors in both a track event and a field event. There was a great deal of pressure on the Houston athlete, and not just because of the articles in the press comparing him to Owens. Lewis had already realized that he was a businessman as well as an athlete, and he knew that he had to position himself in the market. "To make a serious move in my sport, I would need a good spring," he later wrote about this point in his career. "In college track and field, that is a prerequisite course for Introduction to European Money." He had already enjoyed a good spring, but a double victory at the NCAA meet would make the price of his product— himself—skyrocket.

Carl Lewis came into the meet as a celebrity, and so did Carol Lewis, although she was still a high school senior. Just a few days before, *Sports Illustrated,* the most widely read American sports magazine, had done a glowing feature article on the two siblings. Now the whole family was on hand to watch Carl go for the double victory.

Even before the meet began, Lewis experienced what he later called one of the most important days in his life. As he was resting in his hotel room the day before the long jump competition, he had a visit from Willie Gault, a standout hurdler and wide receiver from the University of Tennessee. Over the course of two track seasons and numerous meets, Lewis and Gault had become good friends; when Gault said he wanted Lewis to meet someone, Lewis gladly went along.

Gault took Lewis to see Sam Mings, the founder of Lay Witnesses for Christ, an organization for star athletes who are Christians. According to Lewis, Mings spoke to him about what God had done for the world in Jesus, and what it meant to have a personal relationship with Jesus. Lewis had always been a churchgoer but did not consider himself a deeply committed Christian. Mings's words had a powerful effect on him, however, and he left the meeting deep in thought.

The next day, Lewis won the long jump for his first 1981 outdoor title—although the event was actually held indoors because of heavy rain. Of nine possible attempts in the preliminaries and finals, Lewis took only three jumps, and he still had the three longest marks in the meet, with a winning effort of 27 feet ¾ inch. The first half of his battle was over.

As the meet progressed, Lewis continued to meet with Mings, Gault, and other Christian athletes, including Mel Lattany from the University of Georgia, one of his main rivals in the 100. After he told his family about the Lay Witnesses, Lewis's brothers decided to join the group for prayer, and later their parents and Carol did the same. As Lewis later wrote, "I think our involvement with Lay Witnesses was the final link to bringing our family as close together as it could be."

Lewis's religious awakening did not diminish his desire to win. On Friday, the fourth day of the

Lewis hits the tape ahead of Jeff Phillips (229) and Mel Lattany (45) to win the 100-meter dash at the 1981 NCAA Outdoor Championships. His time of 9.99 seconds was a personal best.

five-day meet, he lined up eagerly in lane 6 for the finals of the 100. Lewis had looked good in winning two heats of the sprint, but so had Jeff Phillips, a hulking sprinter from Tennessee who had beaten Lewis at a dual meet in March. Phillips was lined up next to Lewis in lane 5. In lane 4 was Lattany, whose personal best in the 100 was a mere .04 seconds behind Lewis's. The race would last barely 10 seconds, and the victory would go to the runner who could maintain his blazing speed a fraction of a second longer than the others.

The gun went off, and Lattany bolted to a big early lead. By the halfway point, Lewis and Phillips drew even, then eased past the Georgia sprinter, staying neck and neck to the finish. Somehow Lewis leaned into the tape first. In his autobiography, Lewis recalls the moment of victory: "I held my arms high and enjoyed the victory. I jogged a little, thinking about what I had accomplished, knowing that I would soon be asked to talk about it, talk about it, and talk about it some more." His triumph was complete, and his time of 9.99 was a new personal best. Phillips was clocked a fraction of a second behind at 10.00, with Lattany in third at 10.06. Lewis had matched the Jesse Owens NCAA double in an age when some track followers speculated that the feat would never be repeated.

As Lewis fielded questions from admiring reporters after the 100, he was interrupted by a gratifying call from Joe Douglas. A meet director in Florence, Italy, had heard about the double victory and wanted Lewis there for a race in two days. He was willing to pay Lewis $2,000 to run the 100.

In a few short months, Lewis had developed into one of the top names in international track and field. Having conquered the college ranks, he was ready to face the best that the nation and the world had to offer. ❧

5

"THE BEST, EVER"

Carl and Carol Lewis pose for a photograph during a 1983 track clinic at Willingboro High School. At this point in his career, Carl was already rated by some observers as the best American track-and-field athlete of all time.

THE INVITATION FROM Florence left Lewis almost no time to savor his double victory in Baton Rouge. He flew home to Houston, picked up some clean clothes, and got on a plane to Italy. The meet itself was nothing special. By chance, however, Lewis found himself sharing a room with Steve Williams, his old track idol. For Lewis, this almost made the $2,000 appearance fee seem like a bonus.

Immediately after the meet, Lewis flew home for The Athletic Congress (TAC) Championships, the biggest meet of the year in the United States. In less than two weeks, he had traveled from Baton Rouge to Houston, then to Italy, then back to Houston, and finally to Sacramento, California, the site of the championships. Some fans were wondering if all the miles would dim the brightness of the new star of American track and field.

The conditions in Sacramento on the first day of the TAC meet were hot and dry—so hot that the thermometer registered 104 degrees, and so dry that grass fires on the outskirts of the city were sifting ash on the fans and athletes gathered in Hughes Stadium. But as Lewis left the locker room to warm up, he unguardedly said to a reporter, "I love this weather."

There was also a scorching breeze that created a tail wind for the long jumpers. Blown ahead of his steps, Lewis fouled on his first attempt in the pre-liminaries. On his second attempt, he lengthened his approach six inches to compensate for the breeze. His last four strides still slightly off, Lewis hit the board cleanly and soared 28 feet 7¾ inches. It was the second-longest jump in history, just under seven inches shy of Beamon's record. Because of the wind, however, well over the allowable 2.0 maximum, the jump would not count for the record books—it would only serve to qualify Lewis for the long-jump finals.

The next day, after qualifying for the finals in the 100, Lewis again carefully measured his steps. The weather was hot and dry again, but this time the wind was calm. With the finals of the 100 still ahead, Lewis wanted to make his first jump count. Using the full length of his approach to accelerate, Lewis shortened his last two strides and sprang from the board cleanly, landing at 28-3½. This jump went into the books, and though it was shorter than his previous day's effort, it was still the second longest in history.

However, Lewis was not in any way a sure winner. He had to contend with Larry Myricks, who had long been ranked as the world's best long jumper. Myricks had beaten Lewis eight of the nine times they had met, including every major competition. On his first attempt, Myricks made a respectable leap of 27 feet 3½ inches, but as he landed, his foot came down on his right hand, and his spikes opened a deep cut on his ring finger. "He went for medical help and I went to run the 100," Lewis recalled.

While the 100 is over in the blink of an eye for the average spectator, for Lewis the race was always carefully paced, almost drawn out. Most sprinters explode out of the blocks and then try to hang on. But Lewis had trained himself to run an even race that made him appear to accelerate at the end. Running that day in lane 7, Lewis went out faster than usual, and he was a close fourth after 30 meters.

Evelyn, Carl, and Bill Lewis enjoy an evening out in New York City in February 1983. Enthusiastic and supportive parents, the elder Lewises were almost always on hand to watch Carl and Carol compete.

By the halfway point, he knew he had the race won. His arms upraised as he hit the tape, he won comfortably in a time of 10.13 seconds, finishing almost .10 seconds ahead of Stanley Floyd.

Back at the long-jump pit, Myricks had returned with his hand bandaged. After fouling twice, he was down to one final attempt. Hitting the board cleanly, he nailed the jump. It was measured at 27-8¾: the fifth-longest jump in history, but not enough to beat Lewis. "I hope Larry isn't too down," Lewis said to the press afterward. "It was the greatest long-jump competition ever."

Some fans and reporters could not understand why Lewis had made only one attempt; they had seen one great jump by Lewis and one great jump by Myricks, and they had hoped for something more, perhaps a lofty exchange of jumps that would have threatened Beamon's record. For Lewis, however, the primary goal was to win; in the course of time the records would come, he believed. Each time he competed in both the 100 and the long jump, he increased the wear on his body and the risk of injury. By attempting fewer jumps, he saved himself, both for races later in the day and meets later in the season.

When Lewis returned to Europe later that summer, he was no longer an anonymous American college athlete. On his behalf, Joe Douglas could demand and receive $2,000 from meet directors for each appearance Lewis made, and Lewis received top billing in meet programs. But Lewis found the grind of traveling from meet to meet and country to country very wearying, with different hotels, different languages, and different food every few days. He never went sight-seeing, either; it took too much energy. Finally, Lewis grew so tired of the routine that he faked an injury at a meet in Oslo, Norway, so he could have an excuse to return to the United States and rest for a while. Ironically, he actually did pull a hamstring later that summer, in the Track and Field World Cup in Rome.

By this time, missing out on a few thousand dollars in appearance money was not about to make a large dent in Lewis's finances. After his double victories in both the NCAA and TAC championships, Nike was eager to keep him as one of its contracted athletes. The shoe company signed him to a lucrative deal with a base pay of $200,000, spread over four years, with additional incentives based on performance: for example, he was to receive $40,000 for each Olympic gold medal he won.

Suddenly, Lewis's high school dream was becoming a reality, as the running track became the road to financial success. The victories that provided him with so much emotional satisfaction would also guarantee his well-being. Finally, Lewis was able to buy some of the things—fine crystal, for instance—that he and his high school buddies had admired when they hung out in the New Jersey shopping malls. He even bought a $175,000 house in suburban Houston. When Lewis won the Sullivan Award at the end of 1981, honoring him as the nation's top amateur athlete, the term *amateur* must have sounded comical to anyone who was aware of his lifestyle.

At the end of Houston's fall 1981 semester, Lewis decided to skip a final exam in history. Between his busy track schedule and other classes that interested him more, he had not prepared for the exam, and he thought that somehow he would make it up. According to university rules, however, the F he received for the course made Lewis ineligible to run for Houston. As a result, he appeared in a New Jersey meet as an unattached athlete and reset the indoor world record in the long jump at 28 feet 1 inch. He could not remain unattached indefinitely, however. To run in the prestigious NCAA Championships, he had to be a member of the university's team. With Coach Tellez's help, Lewis arranged to take a makeup test, but Houston's athletic director, Cedric Dempsey, was not satisfied. If Lewis wished to keep running for Houston, Dempsey wanted Lewis to decrease the number of invitations he accepted to appear in meets.

Lewis had to decide which was more important, running for Houston or running for himself. It was an easy decision. Although he stayed at Houston as a student, from then on he would strictly be running for the Santa Monica Track Club, and Tom Tellez would be coaching him privately.

Because of Lewis's performances in Baton Rouge and Sacramento, the press had dubbed him Double Trouble. At the 1982 TAC Championships in Knoxville, Tennessee, he repeated his double victory. Winning the long jump by now had almost become routine for Lewis. His victory in the 100 came almost as easily. In that race, Lewis cruised past Calvin Smith of Alabama and Mike Miller of Tennessee with machinelike ease and won going away.

In 1983, Lewis went virtually unchallenged. He had not lost in the long jump since Myricks had defeated him in February 1981. When Lewis won the 100, 200, and long jump in the 1983 TAC Championships in Indianapolis, he accomplished something that not even Jesse Owens had achieved. Not since the 19th century had an athlete won three national track-and-field titles in the same year.

Lewis coaches young runners at Willingboro High School in September 1983. Though he was now the most celebrated figure in track and field, Lewis was increasingly subjected to attacks on his personality and integrity.

But in direct proportion to his athletic success, Lewis was exposed to attacks on his performance and personality. For years he had celebrated wins in major competitions by raising his arms in victory at or just before the finish line. Some athletes questioned whether he was merely celebrating or also trying to humiliate his fellow competitors. It did not help when meet promoters provided Lewis with limousines, hotel suites, and other perks. Lewis reinforced the impression that he was aloof and arrogant by avoiding other athletes as he tried to focus on a meet.

On a more serious level, Lewis had to confront rumors that he used performance-enhancing drugs, namely, steroids. This charge had surfaced as early as 1981, when his victories in Baton Rouge and Sacramento had catapulted him into the upper echelons of international track and field. Having worked so hard to reach this level, Lewis was insulted by the rumors. Like other competitors, he had undergone periodic tests for steroids and other illegal substances, and he had always tested clean.

With the storm clouds looming on his personal horizon, Lewis flew to Helsinki, Finland, a few weeks after the Indianapolis meet for the 1983 World Track Championships. The Finnish capital, enjoying warm and sunny August weather, buzzed with excitement over the meet. The previous Olympics had been tarnished by the U.S.–led boycott, and the Helsinki meet would thus be the first true world championship that track fans had witnessed for several years. Considering the level of talent present, many felt that Helsinki was about to host the best track meet of all time.

As the meet progressed, Lewis quickly became the talk of Finland—and the track world. First, his time of 10.07 seconds led an American sweep of the 100, with Calvin Smith and Emmit King running second and third, respectively. (The race had been highly anticipated because Smith, running in the high altitude of Colorado Springs, had lowered the world record to 9.93 seconds just over a month before.) In the long jump, Lewis delayed his first attempt in order to cheer teammate Mary Decker on to victory in the women's 3,000-meter run. Then he exploded through the air with a leap of 28 feet ¾ inch. After one more jump—a solid 27-7½—he passed on his last four attempts while coaching fellow long jumpers Jason Grimes and Mike Conley to another American sweep. He knew that his first jump would not be beaten, and he wanted to save his energy for the finals of the 4 x 100 relay.

The U.S. team for the relay was loaded, consisting of Willie Gault and the three medalists in the 100: Lewis, Smith, and King. Everyone in the stadium expected them to challenge the world record—if they could manage their baton exchanges. The spectators had already seen a lavishly talented American

Lewis takes off after receiving the baton from teammate Calvin Smith during the 4 x 100 relay at the 1983 World Track Championships in Helsinki, Finland. Running his anchor leg in an astonishing 8.9 seconds, Lewis led the U.S. team to a world-record performance.

women's team fail to reach the finals when they were slowed by a poor handoff.

Lewis was slated to run the final leg of the relay, known as the anchor leg. Just before the race, he carefully marked with tape his steps for the baton exchange in lane 6. Suddenly he heard a teammate screaming at him from the stands; although the American team had been in the sixth lane for the preliminaries, they were in lane 3 for the finals. Lewis quickly moved his tape mark.

When the gun went off, Emmit King rocketed out of the blocks. Nearing Willie Gault at the 100-meter mark, he screamed, "Don't leave me!" A week before, in a warm-up meet in Sweden, the two had botched the handoff when Gault took off too soon. This time the transfer was perfect, and Gault ripped through the backstretch, launching the American team into the lead. In his exchange with Calvin

Smith for the third leg, Gault swiped once with the baton, missed, then connected on his second try. With the Italian team close behind, Smith had to get the baton smoothly to Lewis.

Leading by about a yard, Smith made a fine handoff. While accelerating, Lewis switched the baton to his right hand, smiled, then pulled away with the power and grace of a thoroughbred to win by five yards over the Italian team, which was anchored by Pietro Mennea, the world-record holder in the 200.

When Lewis first glanced at the scoreboard clock, he thought it read 38.8 seconds, a decent time for any team except this one. Looking more carefully, he saw that the numbers read 37.86. It was a new world record, a first for Lewis.

Lewis jumped about four feet into the air, landing in the arms of his nearest teammate, long jumper Jason Grimes. Soon King, Gault, Smith, and several other teammates added themselves to the celebratory pile. After the dust settled, it became clear that Lewis had run his leg in 8.9 seconds. Because they get a running start in the exchange zone, the best sprinters usually post exceptionally fast times in relay legs; Lewis's time, however, was unprecedented. Because of his excellence throughout the meet, a French sports paper, *L'Équipe*, nicknamed him Superman. But perhaps the most significant tribute came from a writer in *Sports Illustrated*. Commenting on Lewis's three victories, Kenny Moore wrote, "So it's time that Lewis' popular sobriquet, 'The best American athlete since Jesse Owens,' be retired. Among sprinters, and surely soon among jumpers, he is the best, ever."

At the end of the year, the Associated Press named Lewis its Male Athlete of the Year. With the Los Angeles Olympics coming up, he had every reason to hope for an even better year in 1984. ❧

6

A BITTERSWEET TRIUMPH

I MMEDIATELY AFTER THE Helsinki championships, Lewis was again enveloped by controversy. A Norwegian sportswriter, hearing the rumors alleging his steroid use, made a fantastic leap of the imagination and reported that Lewis had tested positive for performance-enhancing drugs. Although Helsinki meet directors dismissed the story as absurd, it quickly spread through the European press, and a few American papers gave it some play.

With that report in the background, another rumor soon circulated to the effect that massive doses of hormones had created a cyst the size of a golf ball in Lewis's chest. According to the story, Lewis required surgery and would be out of action for several months. Desperate for news on the new star of the track world, a few papers also reported this rumor as though it were a fact.

Because of the rumors and the negative comments from some of his fellow athletes, a number of cracks began to appear in Lewis's wholesome image. To a large extent, he was simply experiencing the letdown that naturally follows a huge buildup in the press. Despite the hype, Lewis was not the second coming of Jesse Owens, the legend of sport and sportsmanship; he could only be his own man. If Lewis was guilty of anything, it was allowing the hype to

Lewis demonstrates classic form during a preliminary heat of the 100-meter dash at the 1984 Olympic Games in Los Angeles. After winning his first gold medal in the 100-meter final, Lewis admitted to being "overwhelmed with excitement, joy, relief, all the possible good feelings wrapped up in one."

accelerate. When he failed to conform to the image that the media had built of him, some reporters, whether fairly or not, labeled him as arrogant and self-centered.

On the whole, Lewis tried to ignore the controversies. No one could attack his performance on the track, and he knew he had the support of his family and friends. In addition, he had an ever deepening religious faith that helped him deal with adversity. Ever since the 1981 NCAA Championships, Lewis had taken a leading role in the work of the Lay Witnesses for Christ. While away at big meets, he often spoke to religious groups on what it meant to be a Christian athlete.

By 1983, however, his religious life had taken an unusual turn. Through a close friend, a musician named Narada Michael Walden, Lewis had met an Indian religious leader named Sri Chimnoy, who maintained that athletic fitness was an integral part of spiritual fitness. Although Lewis was skeptical at first, he eventually decided to accept Sri Chimnoy as his guru, or religious teacher. In a ceremony held in a high school in Queens, New York, Lewis received from Sri Chimnoy the name by which other followers of the guru know him—Sudhahota.

Although many Christians would find a dual allegiance to Christ and an Indian guru impossible, in Lewis's mind, there was no contradiction between the two; whether he was reading the Bible or the words of Sri Chimnoy, he believed, his ultimate focus was on God.

Walden also started Lewis on another new path. The musician was producing a record album in connection with the Olympics, and knowing that Lewis had sung in a school choir as a boy and played the cello, Walden asked him to work on the album. After a few voice lessons, Lewis put out a single called "Goin' for the Gold." "We sold some copies on the West Coast," Lewis recalled, "and more in Europe,

Tuning up for the Olympics, Lewis competes in the long jump during a 1984 meet in Sacramento, California. Twice during the previous year, he had jumped 28 feet 10¼ inches, the second-longest distance ever attained.

but we weren't much of a threat to hit the charts." The song never made it onto Walden's album either, but its release opened Lewis's eyes to the possibility of yet another career off the track. At this time, he also took acting lessons in New York and sharpened his communications skills by covering sports for a Houston television station a few hours per week.

By this time, Joe Douglas of the Santa Monica Track Club had become more than just Lewis's track manager. Douglas was also serving as Lewis's personal manager, handling such matters as interview requests and endorsements. Together the two came up with a plan to make Lewis larger than life. Lewis was to be pushed as a personality in as many media markets as possible, including magazines such as *Esquire* that were not usually interested in sports stars. "We want to be loved by all," Douglas explained to *Sports Illustrated*.

Despite his various diversions, Lewis had to remain focused on track, with a long-term view on the upcoming Los Angeles Olympics. With 30 consecutive victories, he had not lost in the long jump in

Lewis appears to be coasting as he wins a preliminary heat in the Olympic 100-meter dash. Despite strong competition in the final, Lewis went on to establish himself as the world's best sprinter.

nearly three years, but in New York's Millrose Games, one of the oldest and most prestigious indoor meets in the United States, he found himself in second place with just one jump remaining. From the start of the meet, Lewis had seemed jinxed. The out-of-date track facilities at Madison Square Garden caused him numerous problems. In particular, the long-jump runway was 13 feet shorter than Lewis's standard 165-foot approach, and it was marred with soft spots and ill-fitting boards that threw his stride off. In five attempts, he had managed no better than 27-2¾, while Larry Myricks had soared to 27-6, his personal best indoors. After his final jump, Myricks was mobbed by the other competitors, who appeared to thrill at the prospect of a Lewis defeat.

Lewis had one jump remaining. But first he had a brief powwow at the top of the runway with Coach Tellez, Joe Douglas, and his sister. They decided that

Carl would start his approach six inches farther back and that Carol would stand next to a particularly loose stretch of the runway boards as Carl raced past, thus giving him better footing.

From 152 feet back, Lewis sprinted down the runway. Narrowly avoiding a foul as he hit the board, he sailed into the air, pumping his arms and legs, and landed deep in the pit. The sellout crowd roared as he bounded from the pit and jumped into his sister's arms, and an even greater roar went up when the distance was announced. Lewis had jumped an astonishing 28 feet 10¼ inches, a new indoor world record. He had made the second-longest jump ever, tying his own mark in the 1983 Indianapolis TAC meet, and he had done it on subpar facilities. Some observers estimated that Lewis's jump, outdoors and under good conditions, could have measured 30 feet. Lewis was inclined to agree, calling his effort "the best jump of my life."

For the rest of the indoor season and the start of the outdoor season, Lewis seemed to win the sprints and long jump almost effortlessly. After the Olympic trials in Los Angeles, where Lewis easily qualified for the U.S. team in the 100, the 200, the long jump, and the 4 x 100 relay team, he appeared poised to enter the realm of myth. No one since Jesse Owens in 1936 had had a better chance at winning four gold medals in track and field. The American public, deprived of its Olympic fix four years earlier by the boycott, was ready to embrace its athletic heroes.

Before the Games even began, however, Lewis came under attack. In *Sports Illustrated*'s Olympic special issue, a feature story by Gary Smith presented Lewis as a talented athlete with the personality of a self-absorbed child. The article ended with Lewis driving away in his BMW after practice: "He pushes a button to open the window, lets the early evening spring air cool his face, and he takes great comfort in knowing he will never die."

In his autobiography, Lewis pointed out several factual errors in the article and condemned it as a work of fiction: "[Gary Smith] wrote one of the best short stories I have ever read. There was only one problem: the person he kept calling Carl Lewis was not me. He was the sloppy creation of a writer who wanted more than anything to write a story that had never before been written." But the truth or falsity of Smith's article was irrelevant. By the time the Olympics rolled around, the damage had been done. Millions of *Sports Illustrated* readers, including hundreds of sportswriters, had a decidedly negative opinion of Lewis as a person, even though they respected him greatly as an athlete.

At the end of July, the world's athletes arrived in Los Angeles—except for the teams from the Soviet Union and its allies, who were staging their own boycott in retaliation for the U.S. boycott in 1980. The pageantry of the Games helped Lewis forget, for the time being, the growing tide of negative press. At the opening ceremonies, he met star athletes from other sports, such as basketball players Michael Jordan and Patrick Ewing. The meaning of the event came home to him when he saw Gina Hemphill, the granddaughter of Jesse Owens, carry the Olympic flame into the stadium, and Rafer Johnson, the 1960 gold-medal decathlete, light the torch itself.

Almost immediately after the opening ceremonies, the media pressure on Lewis began. When he arrived at the Olympic Village, he was assigned with four other athletes to a dormitory room meant for two people. In order to get the rest he needed, he decided to stay out of the village and move into a house with his family. For some members of the media, this move was a sign of Lewis's arrogance and unwillingness to mingle with his teammates.

Lewis did not help his cause by showing up 30 minutes late for his pre-Olympics press conference, even though he explained that the U.S. Olympic Committee had changed the starting time at the last minute. The session itself went well, but the *New York Times*, for instance, reported sarcastically that Lewis had arrived "fashionably late."

Some writers also criticized Lewis for what they considered crass materialism. At the press conference, Joe Douglas said something to the effect that after the Olympics Carl Lewis would be as big as the pop singer Michael Jackson. It was not the first time Douglas had used this analogy. For instance, that spring he had told the *Saturday Evening Post*, "I'd hope he'd be worth as much as Michael Jackson." But the media, following the sentiments of the American public, expected athletes to enjoy success primarily for the love of sport, not for its material rewards. Douglas would later call the quote a mistake. Whether a mistake or not, the Michael Jackson quote gave a strong indication that both Douglas and Lewis were very much concerned with reaping the cash benefits of Olympic gold, and it would come back to haunt them.

Finally, Lewis was able to escape from the hype and compete on the track. He felt good in the preliminaries of the 100, but the finals were loaded. In addition to Lewis's teammates Ron Brown and Sam Graddy, a young Jamaican named Ray Stewart had looked fast in the preliminaries, and Ben Johnson of Canada had come out of nowhere to rank as a contender for the gold.

The final turned out to be a classic Lewis race. Graddy was the quickest out of the blocks, and at the 80-meter mark, it looked as though he had a chance for the gold—until Lewis blew past him to win by eight feet with a time of 9.99 seconds.

For Lewis, winning the 100 was the realization of a lifetime dream: an Olympic gold medal. He later wrote in his autobiography, "I tried to gather my

After winning the gold medal in the 100, Lewis does a victory lap while waving the Stars and Stripes. Rather than viewing the display as an expression of joy and patriotism, some of Lewis's critics accused him of staging a publicity stunt.

thoughts, but couldn't. I was overwhelmed with excitement, joy, relief, all the possible good feelings wrapped up in one. I felt a charge from the crowd that I had never felt before. Or maybe it had nothing to do with the crowd. Maybe this was what it feels like when you reach a goal that has been your constant companion for years."

Jogging through his victory lap, he grabbed a large American flag from a fan in the front row of the backstretch and waved it as he circled the track. Normally, the public and the press loved patriotic gestures of this type. But because Lewis's victory had been widely predicted, a few sportswriters suspected that he had planted the flag in the stands as part of a publicity stunt. After all, they had read in *Sports Illustrated* that Douglas had counseled Lewis to make a show of emotion after big victories. One newspaper even tracked down the man who had handed Lewis the flag; he turned out to be an ordinary fan from New Orleans who had never had anything to do with Lewis prior to that moment.

On Monday, August 6, Lewis returned to the Los Angeles Coliseum and cruised through the preliminary rounds of the 200, saving his energy as much as possible for the long-jump finals that evening. The afternoon was sunny, hot, and humid, but by the evening a fresh breeze had cooled the air over the Los Angeles area. The skies were a deep blue, and the packed Coliseum sparkled with the pageantry of the Olympic Games. In terms of sheer dramatics, the stage was set for a world record, and many in the crowd wondered if Lewis would challenge Bob Beamon's record that night.

Down on the field, Lewis was also contemplating the long jump, but from a different perspective. Confident he could win, he still had strong doubts about surpassing Beamon. Since the Olympic trials, his hamstring had been nagging him whenever he jumped. The rapidly cooling temperature and the stadium's swirling winds would only aggravate his condition.

On his first attempt, Lewis reached 28 feet ¼ inch—a solid, if not magnificent, effort. Among the other competitors, only Larry Myricks had jumped more than 28 feet; given the conditions, Lewis doubted that Myricks would approach 28 feet that evening. Lewis made one more attempt, but his steps were off, and he fouled by running through the pit. Unwilling to risk an injury in the cool evening temperatures, he put on his sweats and passed on his remaining attempts.

Slowly it dawned on the crowd that there would be no world record that evening, and some people began to boo. To casual spectators, Lewis seemed like a bad sport robbing them of a moment for the ages; to the informed track fan, his decision seemed wise. An hour later, when Lewis stood on the top step of the winner's stand while the "Star-Spangled Banner" played, the highly partisan crowd had forgotten its

Holding his fourth gold medal of the 1984 Olympics, Lewis rides the shoulders of the U.S. 4 x 100 relay team. Though his haul of medals put him on a par with Jesse Owens, Lewis disputed any comparison. "Jesse Owens is still the same to me, a legend," he said. "I'm just a person with some God-given talent."

disappointment, and Lewis received a huge ovation. Still, some members of the media were not so easily appeased. TV commentator Frank Shorter, the 1972 Olympic marathon champion, later explained the negative reaction: "If you want to be a legend, you don't play it safe."

Lewis had a day off before the 200 finals, and he used the time to recharge his batteries. First he visited with his family and Sri Chimnoy and then spent the evening at a revival sponsored by the Lay Witnesses for Christ. He called the experience "a great boost to help me through the second half of the Games." The effects became obvious during the finals of the 200, as Lewis led a U.S. sweep, winning easily in 19.80 seconds, ahead of Kirk Baptiste and Thomas Jefferson. After kneeling on the track for a moment of thankful prayer, the three took a loudly cheered victory lap.

On the final day of the track-and-field competition, Lewis anchored the 4 x 100 relay team to the gold medal and a world record of 37.83 seconds, .03 seconds faster than the American time in Helsinki. With Graddy, Brown, and Calvin Smith running the other three legs, the only suspense had been in the margin of the American victory—about seven meters. Upon receiving their medals, the rest of the team hoisted Lewis onto their shoulders and ran a victory lap around the track.

The Olympics were over, and Lewis had accomplished his goal of four gold medals in four events. Again he felt a surge of emotion that mixed joy and relief. When asked about the comparison to Jesse Owens, the last man to win four Olympic golds in track and field, Lewis responded graciously. "My job is just to compete as an athlete and be a nice guy," he said. "Jesse Owens is still the same to me, a legend. I'm just a person with some God-given talent."

At the very least, Lewis had four gold medals that could not be taken from him, in addition to the personal satisfaction that comes with a job well done. His contract with Nike, with its bonus for each gold medal, guaranteed him an immediate financial reward, in addition to the product endorsements he could hope for. But a few gracious words and four gold medals could not repair his damaged reputation. A large segment of the American public had decided that Lewis, with his carefully coiffed hair and flashy clothes, lacked the humility that should characterize an American hero. Whether this view was fair or not, Lewis found himself a generally unpopular man in the midst of his greatest triumph. ❧

7

PICKING UP THE PIECES

F OR THE MOST part, Lewis was unable to exchange his Olympic gold for American green, although a few Japanese companies asked him to endorse their products. Before the Olympics, he and Douglas had been negotiating with Coca-Cola to do a series of advertisements, but after all the negative publicity surrounding Lewis, the beverage giant decided to look elsewhere. Adding insult to injury, thieves had broken into Lewis's Houston home during the Olympics and stolen a number of valuable items while smashing his fine crystal.

Lewis picked up the pieces and finished out the track season on the European circuit, where he was able to command $5,000 per race. In December, the Associated Press named him its Male Athlete of the Year for the second year in a row, a tribute not bestowed on any athlete in nearly 40 years. For the most part, however, the press continued to criticize him. He began to feel that whenever he said anything, the media would present it in the worst possible light.

Even with the support of his family, Lewis found it very difficult to endure the criticism. His father counseled him not to worry about it, telling his son that he had neither hurt anybody nor done anything wrong. "Be yourself, and don't worry about what's

Branching out in a new direction, Lewis makes his television debut as a singer in Tokyo, Japan, in 1985. Though his singing received mixed reviews, Lewis declared himself eager "to explore beyond the limits often placed on an athlete."

going on around you," was his advice. Evelyn Lewis, on the other hand, advocated a more aggressive approach, urging Carl to defend himself.

Finally, in February 1985, Carl decided to vent his anger. After easily winning the 60-yard dash at a meet in Dallas, Texas, Lewis stalked over to a crowd of waiting reporters and briefly commented on the race. Then he spoke his mind. "I want to say one other thing," he told the press. "I have been a bit appalled and a bit flabbergasted by the media's mistreatment of me. But I am going to keep on trucking. I am who I am, and that's who I'll stay, and that's who I'll be. That's all I'll say."

True to his word, Lewis left Dallas without saying another word to a reporter. A few days later, he flew to New York to accept the Jesse Owens Award from the great sprinter's widow, Ruth Owens. After receiving the award during a banquet at the Waldorf-Astoria Hotel, Lewis was asked to make a brief speech. First he paid tribute to the inspirational role Jesse Owens had played in his life and thanked Mrs. Owens for the honor. Then, having had his say in Dallas, Lewis found it in himself to express a few words of regret for the events of the past year. He reminded his listeners about the human side of athletes: "We are people, too. We make mistakes. But we do our best."

Lewis had made a very tentative step toward admitting some responsibility for his negative image. But in an interview later that evening, he was back to blaming the media for his problems, implying that reporters desperate for news had resorted to printing untruths.

A few months later, Lewis badly pulled his hamstring and had to take some time out from serious competition, including half the European season and the 1985 TAC Championships. However, the injury afforded him the opportunity to explore some career possibilities in music and acting.

In a rare second-place finish, Lewis follows Harvey Glace across the finish line in the 100-meter dash at the S & W Invitational in May 1986. Throughout the year, Lewis coped not only with the pressures of competition but with his father's desperate battle against cancer.

With a Houston band named Electric Storm (and the financial backing of a Japanese company), Lewis released an album entitled *The Feeling That I Feel*. If the aftermath of the Olympics had shown that Lewis was not track's Michael Jackson, then this album proved that he was not music's next Michael Jackson either; at best, the reviews were mixed. The album drew enough interest, however, to attract financing for additional recordings. One of them, a single called "Break It Up," hit the charts in Sweden.

Lewis's acting career was even less successful than his ventures into music. The best he could do was a bit part in a movie named *Dirty Laundry*, released in 1987 with little success. Lewis seemed to think he could do anything he put his mind to; many music and film critics, however, advised him to stick with track and field. In any case, he appreciated the experience these diversions afforded him. "Acting and singing had taken me into new worlds," he said, "allowing me to explore beyond the limits often placed on an athlete."

In 1986, Lewis had to cope with a grave family crisis. While visiting Houston the previous Christmas, Bill Lewis had suddenly felt unwell and had returned to New Jersey to rest. After a few days, he visited a doctor, who discovered a cancerous tumor in his colon. In January, surgeons removed the tumor, but the cancer had already spread to Lewis's liver and lymph nodes. In an attempt to arrest the disease, Lewis began receiving chemotherapy, the exhausting but potentially life-saving treatment for many forms of cancer.

Carl's concern for track paled beside his concern for his father, but above all, Bill Lewis wanted his son to keep competing. Thus, just two weeks after his father's surgery, Carl ran the 60 in the *Dallas Times Herald* Invitational. Not surprisingly, he came in second, finishing behind Emmit King, but beating two college sensations, Roy Martin and Joe DeLoach.

DeLoach was no stranger to Lewis. The former Cougar had helped recruit DeLoach to the University of Houston, and now the two often trained together under Coach Tellez's watchful eye. Pushed in practice by the young sprinter, Lewis slowly regained some of his 1984 form. His first big test against the latest crop of young athletes came at the TAC Outdoor Championships in Eugene, Oregon, in June 1986. With his father in the stands, Lewis blitzed through the field to win the 100 in 9.91 seconds, catching Lee McRae of the University of Pittsburgh in the last 20 meters. For a moment he thought he had broken the world record; however, the trailing breeze had been more than double the allowable 2.0 meters per second, so the time could not go into the record book.

Lewis went straight from the track to the long-jump pit, where he unleashed a jump of 28 feet 5½ inches, just enough to beat Mike Conley, who became the first athlete to jump over 28 feet and lose. Although Lewis looked good, it was evident he had yet to regain his old form. The next day, a tired Lewis struggled through the 200 and finished fourth. "It's

Nursing an injured hamstring, Lewis rests during a 1986 meet in San Jose, California. Undiscouraged by his struggles during the season, Lewis said, "I'll do better. And people will understand now that I'm not a robot."

satisfying when people feel I'm a normal guy who has had to work hard to get back to the top after some losses," said Lewis. "An atrocious race like this is good for me. I'll do better. And people will understand now that I'm not a robot."

Perhaps more satisfying than the two victories was his father's apparent return to good health. For a time, the elder Lewis felt well enough to travel with his wife to meets across the country; that summer, they even visited Europe and the Soviet Union. But Bill

Lewis returned to New Jersey feeling exhausted. Soon thereafter, doctors confirmed the worst; despite the chemotherapy, the cancer was spreading, and there was nothing more they could do. Bothered by a knee injury and needed at home, Carl Lewis decided to skip the remainder of the European season and return to the United States.

That fall, Lewis made a point of visiting his father as often as possible. On Christmas Day, 1986, Bill Lewis had a relapse. Unable to eat, he had to enter the hospital, and in early May he died. Carl and Carol were in Houston when they got the news. Carol flew to New Jersey almost immediately, but Carl remained in Houston a day longer to sort out his thoughts: "No matter what I tried to do," he later wrote, "I could only think about my father—the old days in Willingboro, the lessons he taught me, the way he pushed me to always do my best, no matter what I was doing, all the trips we had made, all over the world."

Lewis respected his father more than anyone he had ever known. Without his father's support and love, he doubted that he would have accomplished as much as he had on the track. Now his father was gone. On the way to the airport, he stopped at the bank and took his Olympic medal for the 100-meter dash, the first he had won, from a safe-deposit box. A few days later, when Bill Lewis was lowered into the ground, Carl buried the medal with him as a token of his love and respect. He vowed to win another gold in the 100 in memory of his father.

Soon after the funeral, Lewis dedicated the upcoming outdoor season to his father's memory. "This is going to be my best year," he said, "and my father is going to be there watching it. He's not gone, he's just watching from another place." A few weeks later, in California's Modesto Invitational, Lewis ran the year's best time in the 200. A bigger test, however, came later that summer at the Pan American Games, which were being held that year in Indianapolis. Because Lewis had often jumped well in the city's Indiana University stadium, expectations were high. As usual, some fans speculated that Lewis would finally break the world record. "It's in me," Lewis responded when asked about it. "I know I can jump over 29 feet. The talent is there and I've worked hard at it. But I'm not possessed by the thought of a world record."

On the day of the long-jump finals, strong winds were swirling through the stadium. Nonetheless, Lewis managed a leap of 28 feet 8½ inches, a Pan American Games record. His nagging leg injuries of the year before no longer seemed to be bothering him. Along with his return to form on the track, Lewis found himself on more cordial terms with the press. Joe Douglas had arranged a series of newspaper interviews, culminating in a large press conference just before the Pan American Games, and the media in general found Lewis to be much more accommodating and easygoing. "So it appears the press will, for at least a few more years, have Carl Lewis to kick around," one columnist wrote during the meet. "The question after [the] event here: Will it want to?"

While building one bridge, Lewis was in the process of tearing down another. Over the past two years, his relationship with Nike had become increasingly stormy. Finally, just after his father's death, the shoe company threatened to end its agreement with Lewis, claiming he had violated his contract. Nike charged that Lewis had appeared at sporting events in sportswear that did not carry the Nike logo. After a series of suits and countersuits, the two sides settled out of court. His split with Nike allowed Lewis to sign a lucrative contract with Mizuno, a Japanese shoe company.

These concerns were far from Lewis's mind as he traveled to Rome for the 1987 World Track Cham-

Following his father's death in May 1987, Lewis vowed to honor his father's memory by having his best year ever. Here he sets a meet record at the SAC Relays with a jump of 28 feet 9¼ inches.

pionships. Because most of the Soviet bloc nations had boycotted the 1984 Los Angeles Olympics, the Rome meet was the biggest event since the Helsinki World Championships four years before. Nearly 2,000 athletes from 150 countries were slated to compete. For Lewis, there was only one person standing in his path to glory—the Canadian Ben Johnson, who after a surprise bronze medal in Los Angeles had rocketed to the upper levels of international track. While Lewis had been fighting injuries and coping with the death of his father, Johnson had been steadily lowering his time in the 100.

Lewis looked awesome in the preliminaries, running a 10.05 in the first round and 10.03 in the semifinals almost effortlessly. Johnson, however, had also looked good. In his semifinal race, he had practically jogged through the final 10 meters and still turned in a qualifying time of 10.15.

Rome's Stadio Olimpico was packed for the finals of the 100. The crowd sensed that a world record was imminent. Steadfastly ignoring one another, Lewis and Johnson lined up side by side. They were a study in contrasts. In comparison to the heavily muscled Canadian, Lewis looked lean and lanky. Slowly the sprinters rose at the command to get set, then froze in their blocks, concentrating for the start.

At the gun, Johnson exploded out of the blocks. His reaction was so swift that some spectators expected the officials to signal a false start. The sensors in his blocks, however, had not registered any violation, and Johnson tore like a bull down the track. After 10 strides, he was a full two meters ahead of Lewis, who seemed almost stunned by Johnson's explosive start.

At the halfway point, Lewis began to narrow the gap, moving to within one meter of Johnson. But that was as close as he could come. Unlike most fast starters who struggle at the end, Johnson never faltered. The Canadian's time was 9.83 seconds, which absolutely destroyed Calvin Smith's four-year-old world record of 9.93. Lewis himself was clocked at 9.93. On any other day, it would have been his first individual world record, but in Rome all he could do was shake Johnson's hand.

The crowd roared its approval of the new world record, but shortly after the race, Lewis heard some disturbing news from Joe Douglas. An American women's coach named Pat Connolly had been standing behind Johnson's coach, Charlie Francis, during the race, and she had heard Francis say, "They can say anything to me they want. I'm just going to say that Ben had gonorrhea."

Canada's Ben Johnson sets a new world record as he defeats Lewis in the 100-meter dash at the 1987 World Track Championships in Rome. Following the race, Lewis caused a major controversy when he charged that some leading athletes were using steroids.

These were disturbing words. There were rumors that some athletes used a drug called probenecid as a masking agent for various performance-enhancing drugs. If an athlete were taking steroids and probenecid at the same time, only the probenecid would show up on drug tests. Because probenecid was commonly prescribed for the treatment of gonorrhea, a sexually transmitted disease, there was nothing illegal about its use by an athlete. To Douglas and Lewis, Francis's words clearly implied that Johnson was taking probenecid as a cover for steroids.

Lewis had sometimes wondered if Johnson were using steroids. When Johnson started competing on the international circuit, he was a quiet, relatively mild-mannered athlete. Suddenly he had become boastful, even arrogant, and such changes in temperament were known as a mark of steroid use. Furthermore, Johnson had become physically huge; he was built more like a linebacker than a sprinter. He could have been lifting weights, but usually the added bulk would have slowed him down. Johnson's ability to grow bigger and faster at the same time clearly suggested steroids.

Lewis decided to make a public statement about steroids in track and field. "I feel strange at these championships," he said in an interview with a British television station. "A lot of people have come from nowhere and are running unbelievably." While refusing to name names, he went on to say that some of the meet's gold medalists were clearly drug users.

His comments caused a furor in Rome. Some accused Lewis of being a sore loser. Meet officials, busily celebrating their wildly successful championships, brusquely dismissed the charges. Thus, when Lewis defended his long-jump title and anchored a winning 4 x 100 relay squad a few days later, no one seemed to notice. Rather than praising his success, people looked at the latest controversy he had become embroiled in and wondered if he had once again put his foot in his mouth. •◑•

8

VINDICATION IN SEOUL

Lewis crosses the finish line in a 100-meter heat during the 1988 Olympics in Seoul, Korea, with France's Jean-Charles Trouabal in second place. The Seoul Olympics provided Lewis with a chance to repair the damage he had previously done to his public image.

OVER THE YEARS, Lewis had enjoyed some of his finest moments at the Indiana University stadium in Indianapolis, the site of the 1988 Olympic trials. As the competition began at the end of July, sportswriters speculated that this might be the moment when Lewis would finally break the seemingly immortal long-jump record set by Bob Beamon in Mexico City.

Lewis was more concerned with qualifying for the upcoming Seoul Olympics than with breaking world records, and he had no problems meeting this modest goal in the 100, winning easily with a wind-aided time of 9.78 seconds. By his own admission, Lewis took the opportunity to flaunt his new Mizuno spikes in front of Nike representative Don Coleman, who happened to be sitting in the stands near Evelyn Lewis.

A day later, Lewis turned his attention to the long jump. He had won 33 competitions in a row over Larry Myricks, his number one rival, but Myricks had never wavered in his determination to beat the man who had dethroned him as the world's best long jumper. Making his second jump on the warm, muggy evening, Myricks uncorked a leap of 28 feet ¾ inch to move into first place. Immediately after his jump, though, the angry black clouds hovering above the stadium unleashed a torrential downpour. The tem-

Responding to a powerful challenge from Larry Myricks, Lewis captures the long jump with a leap of 28 feet 9 inches. One sportswriter described the competition between the two Americans as "the greatest long jump duel in history."

perature dropped as the rain continued, and a strong tail wind picked up. Lewis stood at the end of the runway, staring at the pit as if spellbound by the task before him. Then he jumped, landing 28 feet 2½ inches from the board. Bounding out of the pit, he turned and faced the crowd, then raised his arms in triumph.

But Myricks was not finished. After a brief delay because of the storm, he calmly launched himself to a mark of 28-8½. It was the best jump of his long career and put him firmly back into first place.

Lewis later told reporters, "I felt like a boxer in a slugging match." Maintaining the same outward calm as Myricks, Lewis answered the challenge as evening turned to night. On his next attempt, he soared far and to the right, hitting the sand at 28-9. Describing the competition later in *Sports Illustrated,* Kenny Moore wrote of that moment, "No matter what happened now, this was the greatest long jump duel in history."

On his last attempt, Myricks faltered, fouling by six inches, and Lewis's victory streak was safe. Although the two men had not been friendly for years, they could honestly congratulate each other for their sheer excellence. Said Myricks afterward, "Carl was nicer to me this time than he has ever been. I think Ben Johnson brought him down to earth some."

The 200 final later that evening proved that Lewis was, after all, mortal. He went out fast, hoping the cooler temperatures brought by the storm would carry him through to a fast time. But his strategy backfired. His legs weary from two days of races, Lewis faltered on the homestretch, and his Santa Monica teammate Joe DeLoach shot past him to win in 19.96 seconds. Lewis just held off Roy Martin and Albert Robinson to take second place and another spot in the Olympics. Said Lewis, "I went out too hard. When I came out of the turn, I knew either I was going to run 19.6 or die."

A month later, Lewis found himself in Zurich, Switzerland, with the Santa Monica Track Club for the city's annual Weltklasse meet. European track fans were abuzz with the prospect of a possible rematch between Lewis and Ben Johnson. After intense negotiations between the rival sprinters' managers, Weltklasse officials announced that the rematch would in fact take place. According to well-founded reports in the press, Johnson and Lewis would be paid an astonishing $250,000 apiece for the race.

The much-anticipated race took place under ideal conditions, on August 24, 1988. The stadium was packed, the temperature was comfortable, and the day windless. Already the enthusiastic crowd had seen Butch Reynolds of the United States destroy a 20-year-old world record in the 400 with a time of 43.29. If there was one event that might surpass Reynolds's race, it was the most lucrative 100 meters in history.

Johnson and Lewis lined up side by side in lanes 4 and 5 and slowly raised themselves to the set position. Then Johnson broke ranks. Although he claimed that a camera flash had distracted him, officials called it a false start; one more foul would mean disqualification for the Canadian.

The false start was a clear setback for a sprinter known for his explosive starts. Nonetheless, when the gun went off, Johnson shot out of the blocks and quickly surged to a lead of 1 meter over Lewis. After 80 meters, though, Johnson had spent his strength. Lewis eased past him 10 meters from the finish and held on to win in 9.93 seconds, the fastest legal time in the world for that year. Johnson faded to third behind Calvin Smith and finished with a time of 10.0.

Shortly after the race, Lewis heard a piece of upsetting news from Jack Scott, a physiotherapist who had treated both Johnson and Lewis: Johnson's doctor, Jamie Astaphan, had bluntly told Scott that the Canadian sprinter was taking steroids to increase his speed. According to this account, Dr. Astaphan wanted Scott to ask Lewis if he were interested in working with Astaphan and getting on the same "stuff," which the doctor speculated would lower Lewis's time to 9.5 in the 100. Scott knew that Lewis was not interested in any sort of performance-enhancing drug. His news confirmed what Lewis had suspected in the Rome World Championships; if Lewis wanted to beat Johnson in Seoul, he would have to beat an athlete whose speed was anything but natural.

Lewis had five weeks after Zurich to focus on getting himself into peak condition for Seoul. In 1984, he had concentrated on taking four gold medals; in 1988, he was going to maximize each individual performance. If doing his best meant taking every jump in the long jump, so be it. If a victory were to come easy, he would at least not be accused of making it look effortless.

The 1988 Olympics in the South Korean capital of Seoul promised to be the biggest international event in years. For the first time since the 1976 Games, both the United States and the Soviet Union were competing; only North Korea, which refused to cooperate with its southern rival, and Cuba, still a hard-line Communist nation, kept their athletes home.

Eager to confirm its status as a first-class economic power, South Korea was determined to put on a show for the Olympics. Fearing protests or political disturbances, the South Korean government positioned hundreds of police units in the capital, and athletes were whisked to and from the sports facilities amid tight security. The Games opened in Seoul's Olympic Stadium with a dazzling mix of traditional Korean music and dance, high technology, and the pomp and splendor of the Olympics themselves.

Lewis was determined not to repeat the public relations mistakes he had made in 1984. After making his way through repeated security stops, he checked himself into the Olympic Village, then quietly moved to a house that was a part of a Baptist mission, where he stayed with his family, Joe Douglas, and a number of friends.

Lewis speaks at a religious service in Seoul during the 1988 Olympics. Since 1983, Lewis has been an active member of Lay Witnesses for Christ, an organization of star athletes who are Christians.

The first event for Lewis was the 100. As he worked his way through the preliminary rounds, Lewis noticed that the Korean spectators were much noisier than European and American fans; even when the announcers asked them to be quiet at the start of races, they rarely cooperated. But Lewis made up his mind to ignore the constant din of 70,000 people as he strove to replace the gold medal he had buried with his father.

Lewis is stuck in the middle of the pack as Ben Johnson pulls away in the 100-meter final. When Johnson failed a drug test after the race, Olympic officials awarded the gold medal to Lewis, the second-place finisher.

On the day of the finals, Lewis tried to stay focused, but one distraction did get to him. As he shook hands with the other finalists, he caught a glimpse of Ben Johnson's eyes and saw that they were a murky yellow. It was a sure sign of steroid use, an indication that Johnson's liver was working overtime to process some drug that had been pumped into him.

Lewis was nonetheless determined to run his own race, and at the command, he eased himself into the starting blocks. Three lanes to his right, Johnson glared almost angrily down the track.

Lewis knew that the race would be won or lost at the start. If Johnson exploded to a big lead, as had happened in Rome, then the race would be over.

The starter called the runners to the set position, and for an instant, the eight finalists were frozen in their blocks. Both Johnson and Lewis shot out quickly at the gun, with Johnson in the lead. At the halfway point, he led by 1 meter; at 80 meters, his lead had almost doubled. For someone who wanted to run his own race, Lewis seemed fixated on Johnson. Three times he glanced to his right, and each time he saw Johnson pulling away.

The Canadian never suffered the end-of-race fade that had hit him in Zurich. He crossed the line well in front, pointed his right index finger skyward in victory, and glared back at Lewis. Johnson had shattered his own world record with an unbelievable time of 9.79 seconds. Lewis, running a 9.92, had broken the U.S. record, but crossing the line, he looked as if he had been shot.

Lewis tried to be magnanimous in defeat and went to shake Johnson's hand. But as he later recalled, he could only think of two things: he had let down his father, and Johnson had cheated to win. Johnson, for his part, was anything but humble in victory. "I'd like to say my name is Benjamin Sinclair Johnson, Jr., and this world record will last 50 years, maybe 100," Johnson told the press later that day. "More important than the record was to beat Carl Lewis and win the gold."

After the awards ceremony, Lewis returned to the Baptist mission to rest, and his family and friends tried to console him. Narada Michael Walden took him to see Sri Chimnoy, whom Lewis had invited to Seoul. According to Lewis, Sri Chimnoy told him that something was wrong; Johnson's victory did not "register" with him. But whatever happened, Sri Chimnoy said, Lewis must be grateful to God.

Lewis had no time to dwell on his loss. The next day, he was back at the track for the 200 and the long jump. After advancing through two rounds of the 200, he only had a few moments to rest before the long-jump finals. Nonetheless, he took all six jumps; no one would be able to criticize him for not trying in these Olympics. As a result, Lewis had the four longest jumps of the Games. He won the gold with an effort of 28 feet 7½ inches, leading the way with Mike Powell and Larry Myricks to an American sweep.

That night, a telephone call awakened Lewis from a deep slumber. His brother Cleve was calling from Houston. According to Cleve, there was a report on the news wires that someone—probably Ben Johnson—had tested positive for steroids. Lewis and Douglas started making calls, and over the course of the next few hours the story began to unfold. After careful testing and retesting, the urine sample that Johnson had submitted after winning the 100 had been found to contain high levels of stanozolol, an anabolic steroid, and the International Olympic Committee had decided to strip the gold from Johnson and award it to Lewis.

During the next several weeks, Johnson stoutly denied that he had ever used steroids and complained that his medal had been unjustly taken away. But after Canadian officials launched a full investigation of the charges in 1989, Johnson broke down and admitted that he had been on a steady diet of performance-enhancing drugs, administered by Dr. Astaphan, for the previous eight years. After Johnson's confession, the International Amateur Athletic Federation decided to erase from the record books his 100-meter world record of 9.83 seconds, set in the Rome World Championships, and honored Lewis's 9.92 time in Seoul as the fastest legal 100 in history.

Although he had not had the satisfaction of breaking the tape, Lewis won a gold medal to replace the one he had buried with his father. Before Lewis, no one had ever successfully defended the gold in either the long jump or the 100. Now he had done it in both. That night, Lewis addressed a group on behalf of the Lay Witnesses. He spoke about a dream his mother had had on the night before the 100. In the dream, Bill Lewis had told his wife that whatever

Lewis's long dominance of the 200-meter dash was ended at Seoul by his friend and teammate Joe DeLoach (right), who won the gold with an Olympic record time of 19.75; Lewis took the silver.

happened, everything would be all right. "Today," Lewis told the crowd, "we found out that it was."

Lewis still had two events left: the 200 and the 4 x 100 relay. Again, no one had ever successfully defended a 200-meter gold in the Olympics, and from the preliminaries it was clear that Lewis's biggest challenge would come from his Santa Monica teammate, Joe DeLoach. In the finals, Lewis went out hard and was leading at the start of the homestretch. Then, as had happened in Indianapolis, his legs deserted him. With about 30 meters left, DeLoach cruised past him to win in 19.75, a new Olympic record. Lewis held on to take the silver.

Finishing second in an Olympic race was a new experience for Lewis, but if he had to see somebody else above him on the awards platform, at least it was his friend, teammate, and countryman DeLoach. He was disappointed, but it was nothing compared to the disappointment that was to come.

Beginning with the Olympic trials, Lewis had been feuding with Russ Rogers, the U.S. team's sprint coach, over the makeup of the relay squad. With eight world-class sprinters available, Rogers was

Though settling for the silver medal in the 200-meter dash, Lewis looks relaxed and happy on the victors' stand. Lewis's gracious demeanor during the Seoul Olympics won over a number of writers and athletes who had previously disliked him.

trying to develop a rotation that would allow him to use the hottest runners for the Olympic 4 x 100. Lewis felt that Rogers, who was also an agent, favored the runners he represented and was trying to force Lewis and Joe DeLoach off the team. Rogers, for his part, was annoyed that Lewis and DeLoach were often absent from pre-Olympics practices while being paid to run in European meets.

On September 29, the day before the preliminary heats of the 4 x 100, Rogers finally announced the relay roster. It was a compromise of sorts, but a dangerous compromise. For the first round, Dennis Mitchell, Albert Robinson, Calvin Smith, and Lee McNeill would run; in the semis, DeLoach would run in the place of McNeill; and in the finals, Lewis would replace either Robinson or McNeill, depending on which of the two had been weaker in the first round. In this way, six U.S. runners could qualify for gold medals.

Of course, Rogers's plan assumed that the U.S. team would automatically advance to the finals. The Americans certainly had the speed, but with a different lineup in each race, there was a greater chance of a mistake during handoffs. The plan also put a great deal of pressure on McNeill and Robinson, who knew that they had to prove they belonged on the team. In the preliminary race, these two factors combined to produce disaster. As Lewis watched in horror, McNeill pulled away from Smith before receiving the baton, and when Smith finally caught up to him, McNeill was out of the legal exchange zone. After the three other teams protested, the American squad was disqualified.

It was a disappointing end to an otherwise positive Olympics. For a change, no one could blame Lewis for the foul-up. In general, the 1988 Seoul Olympics had absolved Carl Lewis of controversy. When Lewis had previously alleged that some of his competitors were using steroids, some people had accused him of being a sore loser. When Lewis had feuded with Russ Rogers before the Olympics, some people had accused him of being contentious and selfish. But the disqualification of Ben Johnson and the 4 x 100 relay fiasco showed that when Lewis spoke his mind, he generally spoke the truth, even if the truth was difficult to swallow.

More important, the Seoul Olympics helped to restore Lewis's reputation as a sportsman. When Johnson was disqualified, Lewis was neither gleeful nor self-righteous; instead, he issued a statement of sympathy for Johnson and the people of Canada. His self-control impressed at least one sportswriter. "When these bewildering Olympics recede enough to allow us a sense of proportion," Kenny Moore wrote in *Sports Illustrated*, "we may not remember Johnson being found out as much as Lewis being revealed as the gentleman he always has been."

Perhaps his rejection by the public after Los Angeles, the death of his father, his defeats at the hands of Johnson, and the wisdom that comes with maturity had softened Lewis's rough edges. On the other hand, Lewis may simply have learned that Americans prefer their heroes to be a bit more human, with normal human faults and some genuine humility. Perhaps the "new" Carl Lewis was just a better-managed individual, a man who knew when to speak graciously and when to hold his tongue.

In many respects, Lewis seemed as concerned as ever with his marketability. "Everything was much more positive than 1984, and that would help tremendously in the long run," Lewis later wrote of his media coverage in Seoul. Whether the athlete of 1988 was truly a different Carl Lewis or not, he was clearly still obsessed with his public image. ◆

9

"THE GREATEST MEET
I EVER HAD"

IN MARCH 1989, Lewis was called to Washington, D.C., to testify before a congressional hearing on steroid use in the United States. As a result of the Ben Johnson incident, the media had given wide coverage to the problem of steroid use. The public had been alerted to the unfair advantage gained by athletes using steroids and to the serious health risks posed by performance-enhancing drugs: many doctors asserted that steroid use causes violent mood swings, sexual dysfunction, and prostate cancer. As a result, Congress was considering legislation that would ban the importation of steroids by mail from Mexico and Canada. For Lewis, it was a chance to have his say about fighting steroid use in a forum where his words might effect some change.

Lewis told the legislators that although most American athletes did not use steroids, a few did—athletes who were allegedly role models for America's children. To remedy the problem, Lewis suggested that each sport establish an independent drug-testing agency, because governing organizations like the TAC, fearing a scandal in their own ranks, were either unwilling or unable to identify and punish the offenders. At the end of the hearing, Congressman Romano Mazzoli of Kentucky thanked Lewis for his forthright testimony. "I realize that you haven't been

In February 1989, Lewis took time out from a filming session in Los Angeles to speak with reporters about steroid use among athletes.

Florence Griffith-Joyner, popularly known as Flo-Jo, became an international celebrity after her performance at the 1988 Olympics. Her image was tarnished, however, when Lewis and other athletes suggested that she had used steroids to improve her athletic ability. The charges were never proved.

totally without controversy, and some of it deals with your outspokenness. Let me tell you, in a world in which that is a rare commodity, I would hope you are never bludgeoned into a kind of verbal submission. I hope that you are always willing to stand up for what you believe is correct."

Lewis did occasionally mince his words in order to avoid controversy. After the Johnson incident, he had told a group of students at the University of Pennsylvania that Florence Griffith-Joyner, the winner of the women's 100 and 200 at Seoul, was a steroid user. Griffith-Joyner, who had dazzled the world not only with her athletic talent but also with her flashy tights, flowing black hair, and sinewy physique, angrily denied Lewis's allegation. Though other athletes and coaches had made the same charges against Griffith-Joyner, Joe Douglas convinced Lewis to issue an apology, stating that he had no "personal knowledge" of drug use by Griffith-Joyner. In order to protect his star client's new image, Douglas wanted to keep Lewis away from controversy as much as possible.

However, no one could deflect Lewis from his ongoing battle with the TAC, the governing body of track and field in the United States. Lewis believed that the TAC was doing nothing to promote track and field in the United States. To underscore this point, Lewis, Joe DeLoach, and several other Santa Monica Track Club athletes decided to boycott the TAC Outdoor Championships that June, choosing to compete exclusively in Europe.

Throughout 1989 and 1990, Lewis did not run particularly well, although he successfully defended his undefeated streak in the long jump against repeated challenges from Mike Powell. In the sprints, he had to contend with another University of Houston and Santa Monica athlete—Leroy Burrell.

Burrell, like Lewis, had grown up in the suburbs of Philadelphia, in Lansdowne, Pennsylvania. As a youngster, he had watched Lewis win four Olympic gold medals in Los Angeles. When Burrell reached his senior year in high school, Lewis helped Tellez recruit the sprinter to Houston, and the two athletes quickly became training partners and friends. In many ways, Lewis served as Burrell's mentor. But by 1989, Burrell seemed poised to eclipse Lewis in the world 100-meter rankings. Although he could not seem to beat Lewis in head-to-head competition, his fastest time for the year—9.94 seconds—was better than any time Lewis had posted since Seoul.

In 1990, Burrell continued his surge. Lewis won the 100 at the TAC Outdoor Nationals, but only, it seemed, because Burrell had chosen to focus on the 200. Finally, the two squared off in Seattle, Washington, in the Goodwill Games, a sort of off-

Lewis confers with his manager, Joe Douglas, as he testifies about drug use before the U.S. Congress in 1989. After hearing Lewis's frank views, one congressman told him, "I hope that you are always willing to stand up for what you believe is correct."

year Olympics organized by media mogul Ted Turner. In the 100, Burrell leaned at the tape to beat Lewis by .03 seconds. Many track watchers took the race as a sign that Lewis, at age 29, was approaching the end of his career.

A year later, at the 1991 TAC Nationals in New York City, Burrell captured the unofficial title of "world's fastest human" when he held off a late charge by Lewis and won the 100 in 9.90 seconds, breaking Lewis's world record of 9.92. At the same meet, Lewis needed all six jumps to defeat Mike Powell by a fraction of an inch with an effort of 28 feet 4½ inches. Lewis's problem was not really his own performance. He seemed to be running and jumping as well as ever. The problem was that the rest of the world was catching up to him and, in Burrell's case, passing him. Powell, who did not try to hide his personal dislike of Lewis, bluntly declared, "I plan to beat him sometime this year."

On July 1, 1991, Lewis turned 30. He celebrated his birthday by racing in Lille, France. For the first time since the Seoul Olympics, he was matched up against Ben Johnson in the 100. Without steroids,

Johnson lacked his old explosive start, and he faded in the second half of the race to finish in 10.46. Lewis turned in a time of 10.20, but that was only good enough for second place. The victory was gained by Lewis's Santa Monica teammate Dennis Mitchell, who finished in 10.09 seconds. Despite the loss, Lewis felt that he was peaking, and his performance with his Santa Monica teammates bore this out. Twice that summer they broke the world record in the 4 x 100 relay, lowering the mark to 37.67 seconds in Zurich's Weltklasse meet. They proved that, despite the disastrous performance of the U.S. team in Seoul, American sprinters were still the best in the world. At age 30, Lewis was still one of them.

At the end of August, the best track-and-field athletes from around the globe gathered in Tokyo, Japan, for the World Track Championships. With Burrell, Mitchell, and a host of talented young sprinters racing, and Mike Powell jumping, many fans wondered if this would be the meet that put Lewis out to pasture.

His first test came in the 100. The race looked to be a showdown—but not a grudge match—between Lewis and Burrell. As teammates, training partners, and friends, the two men sought to challenge each other only on the track. Burrell could honestly say before the meet, "Our relationship has grown stronger since I began beating Carl last year." To emphasize the personal bond between the two athletes, their mothers were sitting side by side in the stands, watching their sons compete.

As Lewis and Burrell progressed through the preliminaries and semifinals, they were pushed hard by a host of talented sprinters. Lewis had looked phenomenal, winning his quarterfinal heat in a wind-aided 9.80 seconds and following with a 9.93 in the semis, where he finished a few feet ahead of Frankie Fredericks from the African nation of Namibia. Bur-

Lewis jokes with Tom Tellez, his longtime coach, and teammate Leroy Burrell before the 1991 World Track Championships in Tokyo, Japan. Though he had passed the age of 30, Lewis set a world record in the 100-meter dash during the meet.

rell, on the other hand, struggled at first, then pulled himself together in the semis to win his heat in 9.94 seconds, just ahead of Mitchell and Linford Christie of Great Britain.

The 100 finals took place on a glorious evening. As a full moon rose over the stadium, the emperor and empress of Japan took their seats in the stadium. While Lewis was taking his warm-ups, Tom Tellez came over to give him a few words of advice; too often in big meets, said Tellez, Lewis had run his best race in the semifinals. "I will not," shouted Tellez, "have you run your best race in the damn semis here!"

Lewis needed all the motivation he could get. He knew he would have to run the race of his life to win. Lining up at the blocks, he was surrounded by an all-star lineup: Bruny Surin of Canada, Ray Stewart of Jamaica, Burrell, Christie, Mitchell, and Fredericks. But Lewis thought to himself, This time, if someone beats me, he beats me fairly.

When the gun went off, Mitchell went out fast, followed by Burrell, Stewart, and Christie. Lewis started well, but he was still behind. "I'll bet four people broke the world record for 50 meters," he commented later. "I felt great at 60, and I still was about fifth."

As the lead runners began to struggle, Lewis moved through the pack. By 80 meters, Lewis knew he had a "great shot." With 10 meters to go, he was just shy of Burrell and gaining. Crossing the line an instant later, Lewis glanced to his left, saw Burrell a fraction behind him, then looked up and read his time: 9.86 seconds, and it was legal. He had set a new world record.

Without question, the spectators in Tokyo had witnessed the greatest sprint race in history. Six men—Lewis, Burrell, Mitchell, Christie, Fredericks, and Stewart—had finished under 10 seconds. Burrell, in 9.88, had also broken the world record, and Mitchell had completed an American sweep with his time of 9.91. Thinking about his father, family, and friends, Lewis wept as he did a victory lap. "You can't achieve a night like this without so many people caring about you, and you them," he said to the press afterward. "There was my club, my coaches, then our families, Leroy's and mine, the training, the standard Leroy set. I had to rise to that standard. I had to run the race of my life to beat him, and it was close. I'm proud of all of us who ran the greatest 100 in history."

Without controversy, without steroids, without a committee having to strip the record from somebody else, Lewis finally had his record in the 100. Over the years, he had always insisted that records did not matter to him; at age 30, however, he cared a lot about this one.

His meet was far from over. Next on his schedule was the long jump. If the 100 had been an epochal race between two friends with an international supporting cast, the long jump was destined to be an ugly grudge match. In 15 tries, Mike Powell had never beaten Lewis. Indeed, no one had beaten Lewis since

A sorrowful Ben Johnson testifies at a 1989 Canadian investigation into drug use by athletes. Once a national hero in Canada, Johnson became the object of pity and contempt when he confessed that he had used steroids to improve his running.

February 28, 1981, when Larry Myricks had topped him in an indoor competition. When Lewis had beaten him by a half inch on his last jump at the TAC Nationals, Powell had been bitter in defeat; the sheer dramatics of Lewis's repeated victories galled him. In an Italian meet a few weeks before the Tokyo championships, Lewis had withdrawn from the long jump, citing a strained back; for Powell, it was a sign that Lewis was dodging him to preserve his victory streak. Powell especially despised the Santa Monica Track Club, viewing its members as elitists who demanded special treatment on the internaional track circuit while other athletes suffered with second-rate facilities.

Perhaps what vexed Powell the most was the way the press and public seemed to ignore his long-jumping abilities. In 1968, Bob Beamon had set a record that some had thought would last forever, until Lewis had arrived on the scene and persistently threatened to break the mark. Despite his own recent streak of 28-foot jumps and his near victory in New York, no one ever mentioned Powell as someone who might also surpass Beamon.

Thus, Lewis was confronted in Tokyo's Olympic Stadium by an opponent who craved beating him more than anything in the world. The day was warm, humid, and threatening, with a swirling, unpredictable wind. While warming up for his first attempt, Powell was so charged up that he hyperventilated and grew faint. Lacking focus, he jumped a mere 25 feet 9½ inches on his first attempt.

In contrast to Powell's frenetic state, Lewis was a paragon of composure. On his first effort, he calmly hit the board and sailed 28 feet 5¾ inches, a new meet record. Powell managed to settle down in time for his second attempt and soared 28 feet ½ inch, despite stutter-stepping just before the board. On his third attempt, he dropped to 27-2½. His fourth jump was long and high, but a clear foul.

Lewis, meanwhile, looked as if he were jumping in a vacuum that insulated him from the pressures of competition. On his third attempt, aided by the wind, he reached 28 feet 11¾ inches, the longest jump of his career. Immediately, he came back with a majestic effort of 29-2¾, longer than Beamon's record—but the wind was clocked at 2.9 meters per second, again over the allowable limit.

As a few raindrops started to fall, Powell lined up for his fifth attempt. For a brief moment, a calm seemed to descend upon the stadium as Powell approached the pit. Hitting the board cleanly, he kicked through the air, landed, and then exploded from the sand, pumping his arms in exultation. He had made a splendid jump, and with the wind registering a scant 0.3 meters per second, it was going to count. For half a minute, Powell waited nervously while the jump was measured, and then came the announcement: 29 feet 4½ inches.

Powell had broken the unbreakable record. For 23 years Beamon's Mexico City leap had intimidated all long jumpers with its sheer majesty, and now it

Supreme in the long jump for almost a decade, Lewis leaps 29 feet 2¾ inches in Tokyo. This time he finished second, as Mike Powell captured the event with a world-record jump of 29 feet 4½ inches.

had been surpassed. Powell danced around the pit in ecstatic jubilation, then composed himself. He realized that he could still lose the competition, because Lewis, the man who had been challenging Beamon's record for 10 years, had two attempts remaining, and he too was making the best jumps of his life.

"I thought he'd beat me," Powell admitted afterward. "Deep down I thought he'd do nine meters"—the equivalent of 29-6½. But it was not to be. On his fifth attempt, Lewis hurled himself 29 feet 1½ inches, against a wind of only 0.2 meters per second. On his last attempt, with Powell on the sidelines, his hands folded in prayer, Lewis managed an even 29 feet. In the greatest long-jump competition in history, Lewis had made three jumps of 29 feet or more, and still he had lost. His victory streak was over, and the long-cherished record belonged to someone else.

Lewis graciously tried to congratulate Powell, but according to one observer, he could not seem to bring himself to look the victor in the face. Powell, however, could not contain himself. He climbed into the stands and gave his coach a big bear hug. For Powell, breaking the record while beating Lewis, whom he had always viewed as a man with too big an ego, made the victory all the more sweet. Lewis had trouble conceding the enormity of Powell's accomplishment. "I had the greatest series of all time," he said to the press afterward. "He had just one jump. He may never do it again."

The vanquished Lewis had one more chance to shine: the 4 x 100 relay. With the top three finishers in the 100—Lewis, Burrell, and Mitchell—joining Andre Cason, the American team was the overwhelming favorite. In the finals, on the last day of the meet, Mitchell handed the baton to Lewis with a one-meter lead over France, and Lewis sped through the anchor leg to win by three meters. The U.S. team's time of 37.50 was another world record.

Despite the long-jump loss and despite the many great meets he had had in his track career, Lewis could honestly say that the Tokyo championships were the "greatest meet I ever had." In light of his two world records and three 29-foot jumps, for once nobody could deny the truth of his words. ❧

10

AN ATHLETE
FOR THE AGES

ON A JUNE afternoon in 1992, Carl Lewis grimly walked to the starting line on the track in New Orleans's Tad Gormley Stadium. For days he had been fighting what he thought was a bad cold. The virus made him feel weak, and the steamy 92-degree Louisiana heat sapped what remained of his strength. But he was trying to make the U.S. team for the 1992 Olympics in Barcelona, Spain, and the finals of the 100 were about to begin. There was no time for excuses.

Lewis had looked less than impressive in the preliminary rounds. Although he had advanced easily enough to the finals, he had not displayed his patented late surge in any of the races. Instead, Leroy Burrell, Mark Witherspoon, Mike Marsh, and Dennis Mitchell had looked like the top contenders for the sprint team that would represent the United States in Barcelona. Still, Lewis approached the finals with a ray of hope. The relentless heat had debilitated just about everybody in the stadium, from the fans to the athletes, and he had a history of rising to the occasion just when the odds seemed at their worst.

With the seven other finalists, Lewis took his stance in the blocks. At the gun, he shot forward, then almost immediately eased up as a second gun signaled a false start: Witherspoon's blocks had

Lewis's image towers over pedestrians in downtown Tokyo, Japan. Following his spectacular performance in Tokyo during the 1991 World Track Championships, Lewis was primed for the 1992 Olympics in Barcelona, Spain.

Reasserting his primacy in the long jump, Lewis soars to victory at Barcelona. His winning leap of 28-5½ earned him his third straight Olympic gold medal in the event.

slipped. Twice more the runners lined up, and twice more they were called back for false starts. The delays were exasperating for the tired sprinters and especially unnerving for the struggling Lewis. On one of the false starts, he even felt his calf muscles briefly cramp. Finally, however, the gun went off and the runners were cleanly away.

Lewis started well, but Mitchell started brilliantly. At the halfway point, Burrell and Witherspoon began to close, with Lewis back in the pack. Still, everyone expected Lewis to surge. "I thought Carl was going to come at any time," Burrell said afterward.

But the surge never came. Mitchell held on to the finish, with Witherspoon, Burrell, and Marsh narrowly behind. Because of the heat, a head wind, and the false starts, their times were unremarkable. Lewis's time of 10.28 was especially unimpressive. He seemed to sag over the last 10 meters and finished sixth. "I was sure I could do well today," he said after the race. "I thought I would make the 100-meter team."

Lewis would be going to Barcelona, but only as a long jumper and as an alternate on the 4 x 100 relay squad; in the 200, he had looked similarly weak and had also failed to make the team. With Lewis's 31st birthday a week away, some sportswriters speculated that his long run of excellence was finally coming to an end.

It turned out that Lewis had a more manageable problem. His bad cold was actually a sinus infection that had spread to his thyroid, liver, and kidneys. Immediately after the Olympic trials, he began taking large doses of antibiotics, which soon cleared up the infection. A few weeks later, in an Italian track meet, a healthy Lewis beat Burrell and Witherspoon in the 100. His performance in Italy showed that he might well have qualified for the sprint team if he had been healthy during the trials. However, Lewis chose not to look back. Hoping to avoid a repeat of the controversy that had distracted the American team in Seoul, he indicated that he was content to travel to Barcelona as an alternate. "They can win without me," he said.

Mixing athleticism and the folk culture of Catalonia, Barcelona's province, the 1992 Olympics opened with a stroke of brilliant pageantry. As thousands of athletes and fans looked on, an archer shot a flaming arrow into the night sky to ignite the Olympic torch. Because of the breakup of the Soviet Union and Yugoslavia, countries such as Lithuania and Croatia were competing for the first time in decades, some for the first time ever as independent nations. A record number of athletes in their national uniforms paraded through the stadium.

Marching with the large U.S. contingent, Lewis provided a firsthand description of the ceremonies to an Italian television network through a microphone headset. Afterward, Lewis was criticized for this possible violation of his "amateur" status. Hoping to stay out of another controversy, Lewis agreed not to do it again. In any case, the so-called Dream Team of U.S. basketball stars, featuring Magic Johnson, Larry Bird, and Michael Jordan, gave sportswriters more than enough to talk about.

After a week filled with gymnastics and swimming, the track-and-field events began. In the long jump, expectations were high for Lewis and Mike Powell to challenge each other for the gold and possibly set a new world record in the process. The event, however, was a disappointment. In a swirling wind, Lewis jumped 28 feet 5½ inches on his first attempt, but that turned out to be the best he could do. On each jump, Powell fell short of Lewis's mark, reaching 28 feet only on his fifth attempt. Finally, on his last try, Powell soared beyond 28 feet, but he still missed a gold medal by 1½ inches. Although they were still not friends, the two competitors briefly congratulated each other. Lewis's achievement was indeed remarkable: no one else in Olympic history had won three straight gold medals in the long jump.

For track fans, the Olympic sprints were an odd sight without Lewis, who had seemed to own the events for so long. Great Britain's Linford Christie finally broke the American lock on the 100 by taking the gold, but Mike Marsh of the United States won the 200 after his heavily favored teammate Michael Johnson, suffering from food poisoning, failed to make the finals. Lewis could only sit in the stands and watch the proceedings, like any other spectator—until misfortune struck one of the American sprinters. Running in the semifinals of the 100, Mark Witherspoon ruptured his Achilles tendon, and the call went out for Lewis to take his place in the 4 x 100 relay.

Despite the lineup change, the relay squad advanced easily to the finals. After all, Lewis was no stranger to his teammates, having set the world record with two of them—Dennis Mitchell and Leroy Burrell—a year before in Tokyo. He was also quite familiar with Marsh, a teammate on the Santa Monica Track Club. Furthermore, having competed only in the long jump, Lewis was fresh and eager to run.

On the next-to-last night of the Olympics, the U.S. men's relay squad warmed up for the final. The four men had dedicated their race to the injured Witherspoon, and now it was time for results. In previous Olympics, an American victory had been almost a sure thing, but in Barcelona, the gold was up for grabs. The French and Nigerian squads were bursting with talent, and they wanted nothing better than a win over the long-dominant Americans.

At the gun, Mike Marsh raced out of the blocks, brought the United States to an early lead, and handed off cleanly to Burrell. With Chidi Imoh of

Lewis, silver medalist Mike Powell (left), and bronze medalist Joe Greene celebrate an all-American triumph in the 1992 Olympic long jump.

Nigeria drawing even with him, Burrell tore down the backstretch, then handed the baton to Dennis Mitchell. Running the curve, Mitchell made the exchange to Lewis with the United States clinging to a slim lead of only 1 meter.

Switching the baton from his left hand to his right, Lewis took off toward the finish line. "Yes!" he screamed after five steps, overcome by the sheer exhilaration of running once again in the Olympics. His fresh legs sped him toward the finish line as he pulled away from Davidson Ezinwa of Nigeria.

As he hit the tape, Lewis led by seven meters. Looking up, he saw the winning time: 37.40 seconds, a new world record. Bounding with joy, Lewis jumped into the arms of his teammates. A review of the race showed that he had run his anchor leg in 8.8 seconds. "Lewis, at 31," wrote Kenny Moore in *Sports Illustrated*, "may well have screamed down the Bar-

Lewis exults as he crosses the finish line in the 4 x 100 relay well ahead of Nigeria's Davidson Ezinwa, nailing down a gold medal and a world record for the U.S. team. "This was my best Olympics," a joyful Lewis asserted.

celona track faster than he, or anyone else, had ever run."

In Los Angeles, Lewis had won four gold medals with an almost mechanical perfection, yet controversy and bad press had derailed his drive to win the hearts of the American people. In Seoul, Lewis had won two golds and a silver, yet the botched 4 x 100 relay had tarnished the sheen of his medals. In two events in Barcelona, Lewis had added two more golds to his collection. More important, his comeback from the disappointment of the trials had exemplified the spirit of the Olympics, where the sheer joy of competing is second only to the thrill of victory. In 1984, he had appeared to lack that spark of joy; in 1992, he had personified it. "This was my best Olympics," Lewis could honestly say afterward.

At 31, Lewis proved that he was not over the hill. His triumphs at Barcelona stood as the crown jewels of his career. Although he had never attained the stratospheric popularity that he thought possible in 1984, his fellow Americans were finally beginning to accept Lewis as he was: sometimes outspoken, sometimes brash, sometimes gracious, sometimes arrogant, but always a champion.

In his autobiography, Lewis implied that his track career would end in the near future. Long before, when as a high school student he beat the veteran Steve Williams in the Martin Luther King Games, Lewis had vowed not to run past his prime. "For me," he wrote in *Inside Track*, "there will be no Atlanta in '96. Maybe as a fan, but not as a competitor." Later on, Lewis had second thoughts.

When Carl Lewis qualified for the 1996 Olympic Games in Atlanta, critics believed he was past his prime, too old to compete anymore. Lewis struggled to make the finals, barely qualifying in his last jump in the semi-finals. With his jump of 27 feet, $10^{3/4}$ inches in the first round of the Olympic finals, Carl Lewis proved the critics wrong. Winning his fourth gold medal and ninth overall medal, Lewis captured the hearts of every American watching the Olympics. Undoubtedly, Carl Lewis has left his mark as one of the greatest track-and-field athletes. ❧

CHRONOLOGY

———— ❧ ————

1961   Born Carl Lewis in Birmingham, Alabama, on July 1

1963   Lewis family moves to Willingboro, New Jersey

1968   Bill and Evelyn Lewis found the Willingboro Track Club

1971   Carl Lewis runs competitively for the first time in a Jesse Owens meet in Philadelphia

1973   Wins long jump in regional Jesse Owens meet; travels to San Francisco for national competition

1978   Excels as a sprinter and long jumper at Willingboro High School; receives generous recruitment offers from college coaches

1979   Named New Jersey Long Jumper of the Year; wins a bronze medal for the long jump in the Pan American Games; begins freshman year at the University of Houston

1980   Wins indoor and outdoor NCAA long-jump titles; earns a spot on the American Olympic team, which then boycotts the Moscow Olympics; joins the Santa Monica Track Club and runs on European track circuit

1981   Breaks indoor long-jump world record; becomes first athlete since Jesse Owens to win both a track and a field event in NCAA Outdoor Championships; achieves double victories in the TAC Championships; wins Sullivan Award as nation's top amateur athlete

1983   Becomes first athlete in nearly a century to win three events in the national championships; anchors world-record-setting 4 x 100 team in Helsinki World Track Championships

1984   Wins four gold medals in the Los Angeles Olympics; named Male Athlete of the Year by Associated Press for the second year in a row

1985   Accepts Jesse Owens Award; releases record album *The Feeling That I Feel*

1987   Loses 100-meter dash to Ben Johnson at Rome World Track Championships; alleges steroid use among many top athletes

1988   Awarded gold medal in 100-meter dash at Seoul Olympics after Johnson tests positive for steroids; also wins long jump and takes silver medal in 200-meter dash

1989   After Johnson confesses eight-year steroid use, International Amateur Athletic Federation credits Lewis with world record for time of 9.92 seconds in Seoul; Lewis testifies before a U.S. congressional hearing on steroid use

1991   Lewis breaks 100-meter world record in Tokyo World Track Championships, winning in 9.86 seconds; loses long jump to Mike Powell's record-breaking leap of 29 feet 4 $^1/_2$ inches

1992   Wins his third consecutive Olympic long-jump gold medal in Barcelona, then anchors the American 4 x 100 squad to a world record; publishes autobiography, *Inside Track*

1996   Wins his fourth consecutive Olympic long-jump gold medal in Atlanta; wins tenth Olympic medal and ninth gold medal of his career

FURTHER READING

Ashe, Arthur R. *A Hard Road to Glory*. Vol. 3, *History of the African-American Athlete Since 1946*. New York: Warner Books, 1988.

Gentry, Tony. *Jesse Owens*. New York: Chelsea House, 1990.

Lewis, Carl, with Jeffrey Marx. *Inside Track*. New York: Simon & Schuster, 1992.

Moore, Kenny. "Man, Not Superman." *Sports Illustrated*, October 10, 1988.

Pileggi, Sarah. "Going to Great Lengths." *Sports Illustrated*, June 1, 1981.

Smith, Gary. "I Do What I Want To Do." *Sports Illustrated*, July 18, 1984.

INDEX

———— ❦ ————

Adidas, 42
Ashford, Evelyn, 11
Astaphan, Jamie, 85–86, 90
Athletic Congress, The (TAC), 95, 97

Baptiste, Kirk, 68
Beamon, Bob, 12, 15, 27–29, 44, 51, 67, 83, 102, 103
Birmingham, Alabama, 19, 20
"Break It Up," 73
Brown, Ron, 65, 69
Burrell, Leroy, 97, 98, 99–101, 105, 107–8, 110–11

Cason, Andre, 105
Cheeseborough, Chandra, 11
Christie, Linford, 100–101
Civil rights movement, 20
Conley, Mike, 55, 74

Dallas Times Herald Invitational, 74
Decker, Mary, 11
DeLoach, Joe, 74, 84, 91, 92, 97
Dirty Laundry, 73
Double-hitch kick method, 40, 43–44
Douglas, Joe, 42, 47, 52, 61, 62, 65, 66, 77, 79–80, 87, 90, 96

Electric Storm, 73
Esquire, 61
European track circuit, 42–43, 44, 47, 49, 51, 52, 71, 72, 85, 92, 97

Feeling That I Feel, The, 73
Floyd, Stanley, 43, 50
Francis, Charlie, 79–80
Fredericks, Frankie, 99–101

Gault, Willie, 45, 55–57
"Goin' for the Gold," 60–61
Goodwill Games, 1990, 97–98
Graddy, Sam, 65, 69
Griffith-Joyner, Florence, 96, 97
Grimes, Jason, 55–57

"Hang" jumpers, 39–40
Hines, Jim, 12
Houston, Texas, 11, 39, 49, 71, 73, 74, 76, 90

Inside Track, 17, 34, 35, 46, 64, 113
International Amateur Athletic Federation, 90
International Olympic Committee, 90

Jefferson, Thomas, 68
John F. Kennedy High School, 21
Johnson, Ben, 65, 78–81, 84–86, 88–89, 90, 93, 95, 96, 98
Johnson, Rafer, 27, 64

King, Emmit, 13, 55–57, 74
King, Martin Luther, Jr., 21

Lattany, Mel, 45–47
Lay Witnesses for Christ, 45, 60, 68, 90
Lewis, Bill (father), 13, 19, 20, 21, 22, 23, 31, 34, 41, 45, 71, 74, 75–76, 77, 87, 89, 93, 101
Lewis, Carl
   acting career, 73
   autobiography, 17, 34, 35, 46, 64, 113
   awards, 43, 52, 57, 71, 72
   birth, 19, 20
   childhood, 20–37

college career, 36, 39–53
education, 32, 39
finances, 39, 42–43, 44, 47, 52, 69, 71, 77, 83
4 x 100 relay, 55–57, 63, 69, 81, 91–93, 99, 105, 108, 110–11
injuries, 36, 39, 40, 52, 72
long jump, 11, 12, 15, 16, 17, 22, 31, 33, 35, 36, 39–40, 41, 42, 43, 44, 45, 49, 50–51, 53, 55, 61–63, 67–68, 74, 81, 83–84, 89–90, 97, 98, 99, 101–5, 108, 109–10
music career, 60–61, 73
national champion in three events, 16
NCAA Championships, 40–41, 42, 44–47, 49, 52
Olympic gold medals, 17, 65–69, 89–90, 109–10, 111, 112
100-meter dash, 11, 12, 13, 16, 35, 37, 46–47, 50–51, 53, 55, 63, 65–66, 74, 78–79, 83, 85, 87–89, 90, 97, 98, 99–101, 107–8
Jesse Owens, comparisons with, 41, 44, 47, 53, 57, 59, 69
Jesse Owens, meets, 23, 31
public image problems, 16, 17, 54, 59–60, 63–65, 66, 69, 71, 72, 77, 81, 93, 112
and religion, 45, 60, 68, 90
and steroids, 54–55, 59, 79–81, 86, 90, 93, 95–97, 101
as Sudhahota, 60
Sullivan Award, wins, 52

200-meter dash, 11, 12, 13, 15, 16, 17, 53, 63, 67, 68–69, 75, 77, 84, 89, 91, 108
world records, 17, 57, 63, 90, 98, 99, 101, 105, 110, 111
Lewis, Carol (sister), 13, 20, 22, 23, 32, 41, 42, 44, 45, 62, 63, 76
Lewis, Cleveland (brother), 20, 21, 22–23, 43, 45, 90
Lewis, Evelyn Lawler (mother), 13, 19, 21, 22, 23, 34, 35, 37, 41, 45, 72, 76, 83, 90, 99
Lewis, Mack (brother), 20, 21, 22, 43, 45

McNeill, Lee, 92
McRae, Lee, 74
McTear, Houston, 37
Marino, Patsy, 35
Marsh, Mike, 107–8, 110
Martin, Roy, 74
Martin Luther King Games, 37, 113
Mazzoli, Romano, 95–96
Mennea, Pietro, 16, 57
Miller, Mike, 53
Millrose Games, 62–63
Mings, Sam, 45
Mitchell, Dennis, 92, 99, 100–101, 105, 107–8, 110–11
Mizuno, 77, 83
Modesto Invitational, 12, 76–77
Moore, Kenny, 57
Moses, Edwin, 11, 17
Myricks, Larry, 17, 42, 50, 51, 53, 62, 67, 83–84, 90, 102

National Collegiate Athletic Association (NCAA), 37
NCAA Indoor Championships
1980, 40
1981, 44
NCAA Outdoor Championships
1980, 40–41

1981, 44–47, 52, 60
New Jersey Grand Championship, 37
New York Times, 65
Nike, 42, 43, 52, 77, 83

Olympic Committee, U.S., 65
Olympics, 17
1936, 25–27
1960, 27
1968, 12, 16, 27–29
1980, 41
1984, 57, 61, 64–69, 78, 97, 112
1988, 86–93, 112
1992, 107, 109–12, 113
1996, 113
Owens, Jesse, 23–27, 29, 31, 44, 47, 53, 57, 59, 63, 72
Owens, Ruth, 72

Pan American Games, 20, 39, 77
Patella tendinitis, 36, 39, 40
Phillips, Jeff, 46–47
Powell, Mike, 90, 97, 98, 99, 102–5, 109–10
Probenecid, 80

Reynolds, Butch, 85
Robinson, Albert, 92
Rogers, Russ, 91, 92, 93
Rudolph, Wilma, 27

Santa Monica Track Club, 42, 53, 61, 84, 85, 91, 97, 99, 102, 110
Saturday Evening Post, 65
Scott, Jack, 85–86
Shorter, Frank, 68
16th Street Baptist Church, 20
Smith, Calvin, 53, 55, 69, 79, 84, 92
Smith, Gary, 63–64

Southwest Conference Championship, 44
Spartakiade Games, 1979, 39
Sports Illustrated, 44, 57, 61, 63, 66, 83, 93, 111
Sri Chimnoy, 60, 68, 89
Stanozolol, 90
Steroids, 54–55, 59, 79–81, 85–86, 90, 93, 95–97, 101
Stewart, Ray, 65, 100–101
Surin, Bruny, 100–101

TAC Championships
1981, 49–51, 53
1982, 53
1983, 11–17, 53, 63
1985, 72
1986, 74
1989, 97
1990, 97
1991, 98, 102
Tellez, Tom, 13, 37, 39–40, 42, 53, 62, 74, 97, 100
Track and Field World Cup, 1981, 52
Tuskegee Institute, 19, 20

USA/Mobil Outdoor Track and Field Championships, 1983, 11–17. *See also* TAC Championships
University of Houston, 37, 39, 41, 42, 43, 44, 52, 53, 74, 97

Walden, Narada Michael, 60
Williams, Steve, 37, 49, 113
Willingboro, New Jersey, 21, 76
Willingboro High School, 21, 34, 35
Willingboro Track Club, 22, 23, 32
Witherspoon, Mark, 107–8, 110
World Track Championships
1983, 55–57, 59, 78
1987, 78–81, 86, 88, 90
1991, 99–105, 110

PICTURE CREDITS

STEVE KLOTS, a native of Tennessee, holds a bachelor of arts degree from Trinity College in Connecticut and a master of divinity degree from Harvard University. He has also done postgraduate work studying the role of religion in society at Otago University in Dunedin, New Zealand. The author of four other Chelsea House books, *Richard Allen, Ralph Bunche, Ida Wells-Barnett,* and *Muhammad,* he is currently living and working in Massachusetts as a writer and minister.

NATHAN IRVIN HUGGINS, one of America's leading scholars in the field of black studies, helped select the titles for the BLACK AMERICANS OF ACHIEVEMENT series, for which he also served as senior consulting editor. He was the W.E.B. Du Bois Professor of History and of Afro-American Studies at Harvard University and the director of the W.E.B. Du Bois Institute for Afro-American Research at Harvard. He received his doctorate from Harvard in 1962 and returned there as a professor in 1980 after teaching at Columbia University, the University of Massachusetts, Lake Forest College, and the California State University, Long Beach. He was the author of four books and dozens of articles, including *Black Odyssey: The Afro-American Ordeal in Slavery, The Harlem Renaissance,* and *Slave and Citizen: The Life of Frederick Douglass,* and was associated with the Children's Television Workshop, National Public Radio, the Boston Athenaeum, the Museum of Afro-American History, the Howard Thurman Educational Trust, and Upward Bound. Professor Huggins died in 1989, at the age of 62, in Cambridge, Massachusetts.